Homosexuality

Other Books of Related Interest:

At Issue Series
AIDS in Developing Countries
Transgendered People

Current Controversy Series
Homosexuality

Global Viewpoints Series
Women's Rights

Introducing Issues with Opposing Viewpoints Series
Civil Liberties
Gay Marriage
Homosexuality
Human Rights
Women's Rights

Issues on Trial Series
Gender
Sexual Discrimination

Opposing Viewpoints Series
The Armed Forces
The Catholic Church

Perspectives On Diseases & Disorders Series
AIDS

Social Issues Firsthand Series
AIDS

GLOBALVIEWPOINTS

Homosexuality

Noah Berlatsky, Book Editor

GREENHAVEN PRESS
A part of Gale, Cengage Learning

GALE
CENGAGE Learning

Detroit • New York • San Francisco • New Haven, Conn • Waterville, Maine • London

Christine Nasso, *Publisher*
Elizabeth Des Chenes, *Managing Editor*

© 2011 Greenhaven Press, a part of Gale, Cengage Learning

Gale and Greenhaven Press are registered trademarks used herein under license.

For more information, contact:
Greenhaven Press
27500 Drake Rd.
Farmington Hills, MI 48331-3535
Or you can visit our Internet site at gale.cengage.com

Articles in Greenhaven Press anthologies are often edited for length to meet page requirements. In addition, original titles of these works are changed to clearly present the main thesis and to explicitly indicate the author's opinion. Every effort is made to ensure that Greenhaven Press accurately reflects the original intent of the authors. Every effort has been made to trace the owners of copyrighted material.

Cover image by David Ramos/Getty Images.

LIBRARY OF CONGRESS CATALOGING-IN-PUBLICATION DATA

Homosexuality / Noah Berlatsky, book editor.
   p. cm. -- (Global viewpoints)
   Includes bibliographical references and index.
   ISBN 978-0-7377-5191-8 (hbk.) -- ISBN 978-0-7377-5192-5 (pbk.)
   1. Homosexuality--Juvenile literature. I. Berlatsky, Noah.
   HQ76.25.H67393 2011
   306.76'6--dc22

                                          2010032976

Printed in the United States of America
2 3 4 5 6   16 15 14 13 12

FD194

Contents

Chapter 1: Homosexuality and Religion

Chapter 2: Attitudes Toward Homosexuality

Chapter 3: Homosexuality and the Law

Christian and Muslim Ugandans support a new bill that would bolster the protection of the traditional African heterosexual marriage and provide the death penalty for those convicted of homosexual sex with a minor or while being HIV positive. Several Western governments, human rights groups, and gay activists oppose the bill.

To combat AIDS, the Mexican government has adopted the strategy of promoting tolerance for homosexuals in the hopes that they will be more willing and able to seek and receive treatment if they are HIV positive.

Chapter 4: Homosexuality and Family

In Canada, same-sex marriage has not weakened the institution of marriage, nor increased polygamy, nor resulted in persecution of religious institutions. In general, none of the dire consequences predicted by opponents of same-sex marriage have come to pass in Canada.

Foreword

> *"The problems of all of humanity can only be solved by all of humanity."*
> *—Swiss author Friedrich Dürrenmatt*

Global interdependence has become an undeniable reality. Mass media and technology have increased worldwide access to information and created a society of global citizens. Understanding and navigating this global community is a challenge, requiring a high degree of information literacy and a new level of learning sophistication.

Building on the success of its flagship series, *Opposing Viewpoints*, Greenhaven Press has created the *Global Viewpoints* series to examine a broad range of current, often controversial topics of worldwide importance from a variety of international perspectives. Providing students and other readers with the information they need to explore global connections and think critically about worldwide implications, each *Global Viewpoints* volume offers a panoramic view of a topic of widespread significance.

Drugs, famine, immigration—a broad, international treatment is essential to do justice to social, environmental, health, and political issues such as these. Junior high, high school, and early college students, as well as general readers, can all use *Global Viewpoints* anthologies to discern the complexities relating to each issue. Readers will be able to examine unique national perspectives while, at the same time, appreciating the interconnectedness that global priorities bring to all nations and cultures.

Material in each volume is selected from a diverse range of sources, including journals, magazines, newspapers, nonfiction books, speeches, government documents, pamphlets, organization newsletters, and position papers. *Global Viewpoints* is truly global, with material drawn primarily from international sources available in English and secondarily from U.S. sources with extensive international coverage.

Features of each volume in the *Global Viewpoints* series include:

- An **annotated table of contents** that provides a brief summary of each essay in the volume, including the name of the country or area covered in the essay.

- An **introduction** specific to the volume topic.

- A **world map** to help readers locate the countries or areas covered in the essays.

- For each viewpoint, an **introduction** that contains notes about the author and source of the viewpoint explains why material from the specific country is being presented, summarizes the main points of the viewpoint, and offers three **guided reading questions** to aid in understanding and comprehension.

- **For further discussion** questions that promote critical thinking by asking the reader to compare and contrast aspects of the viewpoints or draw conclusions about perspectives and arguments.

- A worldwide list of **organizations to contact** for readers seeking additional information.

- A **periodical bibliography** for each chapter and a **bibliography of books** on the volume topic to aid in further research.

- A comprehensive **subject index** to offer access to people, places, events, and subjects cited in the text, with the countries covered in the viewpoints highlighted.

Global Viewpoints is designed for a broad spectrum of readers who want to learn more about current events, history, political science, government, international relations, economics, environmental science, world cultures, and sociology—students doing research for class assignments or debates, teachers and faculty seeking to supplement course materials, and others wanting to understand current issues better. By presenting how people in various countries perceive the root causes, current consequences, and proposed solutions to worldwide challenges, *Global Viewpoints* volumes offer readers opportunities to enhance their global awareness and their knowledge of cultures worldwide.

Introduction

"Though awareness of [homosexuality] has existed throughout the ages, it has been at various times quietly accepted and winked at ('You know, he's that way") or railed against, depending on the circumstances.'

—Allan Laurence Brooks,
in ETC.: A Review of General
Semantics, *July 1, 2009*

Homosexuality today is a controversial issue worldwide. The debate about homosexuality is often framed in terms of rights, identities, and religious principles. However, this has not always been the case. Instead, attitudes and cultural traditions around homosexuality have varied widely from era to era and from place to place.

In certain parts of ancient Greece, especially Athens, homosexuality within certain contexts appears to have been common and accepted. Scholars believe that homosexuality was not seen as an identity the way it is today; instead, many men participated in sexual relationships with both males and females. (Information about lesbian relationships is very scarce.) Furthermore, "the relationship that was characteristic of the Greek way of life, accepted or even regarded as a social duty by the state, was intergenerational male love," according to a February 2000 article on the website The World History of Male Love. In other words, most homosexual relationships were between a grown man and an adolescent boy—a relationship that is often referred to today as pederasty.

An Athenian man had a responsibility to marry a wife and father a child. But he may also have had a responsibility to take a younger male lover who he would "help on his way to manhood and maturity, and to initiate him in the customs of grown-up people," according to Hein van Dolen in an article on Livius.org—though van Dolen also says that the educational aspects of the relationship may have been overstated by some historians.

In any case, educative or not, traditionally the older man was supposed to be the active partner in anal sex, while the adolescent would be the penetrated or passive partner. Van Dolen notes, however, that pederasty was not the only homosexual relationship in Greece. "It was," van Dolen says, "certainly shameful when a man with a beard remained passive . . . and it was even worse when a man allowed himself to be penetrated by another grown-up man." Despite being frowned upon in some sources, however, such relationships apparently did occur, and may even have been fairly common.

The Greek tradition of pederasty had a parallel in Japanese history. "A feature of pre-modern Japanese culture was that male homosexual relations were required to be between a man and a boy, called a *wakashu*. When a wakashu reached the age of nineteen, he underwent a coming-of-age ceremony that conferred on him the status of adult male, after which he took the adult role in relations with boys," according to Paul Gordon Schalow in his 1990 introduction to Ihara Saikaku's classic collection of short stories, *The Great Mirror of Male Love*. Schalow explains that, as in Greece, pederasty in Japan was not stigmatized, though "it was practiced by only a minority of men, and thus required defense vis-à-vis female love."

According to Dirk Deppey in a June 10, 2010, essay on the website of the *Comics Journal*, "I'm aware of only one real, unambiguous example of a pre-modern set of cultures that has dealt with homosexuality through any avenue other than pederasty: Many Native American tribes practiced what was initially known to Westerners as the 'berdache' tradition, and later as the two-spirit tradition. Put simply: Prior to the arrival of Westerners on the North American continent, an estimated two-thirds of aboriginal American tribes dealt with homosexuals through a variety of cross-gender rituals, in which feminine boys and [in some cases] masculine girls would be declared to possess the souls of the opposite gender, and would undergo a variety of tests and ceremonies to reposition them as members of said gender for social purposes." Deppey goes on to note that "to be declared Two-Spirited was to be invited into the tribe to a degree that would have been unimaginable to the Japanese, Greeks, Arabs or virtually any other culture on Earth prior to the 20th century."

Some Native American communities are working to revive the two-spirit tradition. A panelist of the Two Spirit Society of Denver explained, "Even as a kid I was a mediator between the sexes, between genders. . . . I can lay cement and shingle a roof with the best of them. I can also wear a suit and high heels with the best of them," as quoted in a January 30, 2009, post on Feministing.com. In contrast to Deppey, the writer on Feministing.com argues that gender variance such as that represented by the two-spirit tradition was common among indigenous cultures, and has been erased by European colonization.

However, there has also been a varied history of attitudes toward homosexuality in European cultures. For instance, during the 1800s, close, sensual attractions between women in America and Europe were both common and accepted. "[I]t was almost impossible to study the correspondence or literary efforts of nineteenth-century women in America (and elsewhere) without finding some indication that passionate love shared with other women had been typical of their experience at one time or another. And nowhere did it appear that there was a hint of wrongdoing in this, nor that it might be considered abnormal. Furthermore, there were names for it— Boston marriage, romantic friendship, or the love of kindred spirits," according to Elizabeth J. Davenport writing about Lillian Faderman's 1998 book *Surpassing the Love of Men* on the website of the *International Gay & Lesbian Review*. Davenport notes that some women who experienced these romantic friendships even eloped with each other. Usually they were quickly captured and separated by their families, but sometimes not. Sarah Ponsonby and Eleanor Butler ran away together as young women and then "managed to live fifty-three years of apparent wedded bliss thereafter on a small stipend from their families."

In the viewpoints that follow, authors express varied opinions about homosexuality in chapters titled Homosexuality and Religion, Attitudes Toward Homosexuality, Homosexuality and the Law, and Homosexuality and Family. The authors demonstrate the many ways in which different cultures and countries talk about and treat homosexuality.

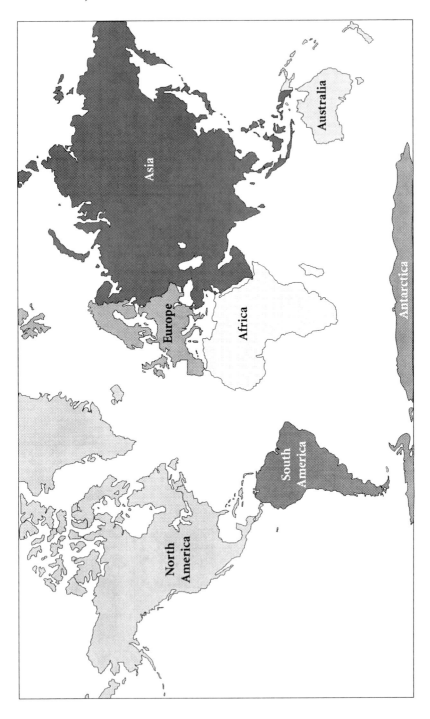

GLOBALVIEWPOINTS

Homosexuality and Religion

Thai Buddhism Has No Clear Teachings on Homosexuality

Hakan Jakob Kosar

Hakan Jakob Kosar is a Danish journalist who worked as an intern on the northern Thai magazine Citylife Chiang Mai. *In the following viewpoint, he describes his efforts as a European to discover Thai Buddhist attitudes toward homosexuality. He concludes that in some cases, Thai Buddhism might equate homosexuality with sexual misconduct or with increased suffering; in other cases, it might not. Since Buddhist traditions and scripture do not appear to discuss homosexuality explicitly, Kosar asserts, the religion does not seem to have one clear position on the subject.*

As you read, consider the following questions:

1. What is "Monk Chat" and where is it held, according to the viewpoint?
2. What does Thuriya say about monogamous homosexual relationships?
3. Why does Somwang Kaewsufong say that the Buddha's views on homosexuality are not "gay hating"?

I am quite new to Thailand—only 30 days have gone by since I put my feet on Thai soil and everything is still mystifying, bewildering, and puzzling to me. The small smoke-

Hakan Jakob Kosar, "The Gay Precept: How Buddhism Views Homosexuality," *Citylife Chiang Mai*, vol. 18, no. 10, October 10, 2009. Reproduced by permission.

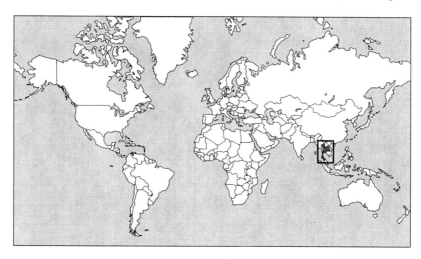

filled spirit houses containing tiny shots of Sang Som [a Thai rum]; the pretty ladies who aren't really ladies [Thailand is known for its cultural acceptance of transgendered individuals, or kathoeys]; the fried creepy crawlies people wolf down with gusto; and the ubiquitous temples, sparkling and spellbinding. But most of all, I am intrigued by the hordes of tonsured, saffron-clad males of all ages and sizes who wander the city carrying their batras (charity bowls). This month [October 2009], *Citylife* is featuring a Pink Issue [focusing on gay issues], and as an intern I had to come up with a relevant feature. So the other day, while getting lost in small alleys, I came across a monk and immediately wondered what he thought of the whole Pink Issue? Indeed, how does Buddhism view homosexuality?

Homosexuality as Sexual Misconduct

I grew up in Europe and since I am part Danish/part Turkish, I was raised with the Abrahamitic monotheistic faiths and their views on homosexuality. Mom was semi-Christian; dad, a very moderate Muslim. Both faiths pretty much express that falling for a person, who has the same 'equipment' as yourself is a *big* no-no! But what did The Awakened One say about the matter? Being an aspiring investigative journalist, I decided to probe the waters and seek the Buddhists' view on homosexuality.

I did some studying on my own but I could not unearth any Buddhist scriptures on the subject. And since the primary source is out of my reach, I went to 'Monk Chat', an event held at Wat Suan Dok [a fourteenth-century temple outside the city of Chiang Mai in northern Thailand] three times a week. Here you—indeed anyone—can ask a follower of the faith questions about their religious convictions. I took a seat in front of Thuriya, a 26-year-old Burmese monk who has worn the cloak [that is, been a monk] for 13 years. Thuriya is a Theravada Buddhist. This is the oldest branch of the faith and perhaps the closest you can get to the original foundation—at least according to some scholars. The robust fellow held my eyes with an intense, almost scrutinising gaze, when I asked him if Siddhartha [Gautama, a spiritual leader who founded Buddhism in India] ever talked about homosexuality.

"In the time of the Buddha, there were no homosexuals, so our great teacher did not mention anything about this; hence it is difficult to discuss the subject from a Buddhist point of view. But I must say that the contemporary Buddhist stance is that it is not acceptable, since it is sexual misconduct," Thuriya explained—after a long silence.

I could sense that he was somewhat uncomfortable discussing the matter even though he reassured me that this was an open conversation. I decided to dig a little deeper and asked him how he would explain why some people feel attracted to a person of the same gender.

"Well, if you, in one of your existences, do not succeed in refraining from sexual misconduct, this can lead to bad karma regarding your sexual condition. Because of this, in a subsequent life, you might be reincarnated as neither a real man, nor a woman, but a homosexual—an 'in between'," he continued.

I have read that Buddhists do not believe in sin, but cause and effect. And I know that Buddha was mostly concerned with suffering, and the means by which you can end suffering and reach enlightenment. A part of the solution is to keep from breaking the five (or sometimes eight) precepts. You should not kill, steal, be promiscuous, lie or intoxicate your mind. Thuriya had mentioned that homosexuality, in his faith, was perceived as sexual misconduct or promiscuity. So I wondered if all homosexual relationships were perceived this way . . . even the monogamous ones.

"Well, that is a difficult question. As I see it, if for instance, two men are in a monogamous relationship, it might not be bad karma or a break of the precept regarding sexual misconduct. But I am not sure," the monk told me.

"In the time of the Buddha, there were no homosexuals, so our great teacher did not mention anything about this."

Homosexuality May Increase Suffering

Being a total novice regarding this belief system, I accepted the explanation from the sincere monk. But still, I wondered, was this a pure account or was it somewhat biased due to Thai culture. I therefore ventured to Chiang Mai University to get the academic interpretation. I was greeted by a lecturer in philosophy and religion, Somwang Kaewsufong, a neat looking man, who radiated intellectualism. He confirmed that Buddha never really touched upon the matter according neither to tradition nor to scriptures. The lecturer then went on to elaborate on Thuriya's exposition regarding why homosexuality could be caused by bad karma:

This might sound sexist to you, but in Buddhism the highest physical state one can be reborn into is that of a man. This is because only a 'natural' man can reach enlighten-

Buddhism Encourages Tolerance

Theravada Buddhist [the oldest surviving branch of Buddhism] countries like Sri Lanka and Burma had no legal statutes against homosexuality between consenting adults until the colonial era when they were introduced by the British. Thailand, which had no colonial experience, still has no such laws. This had led some Western homosexuals to believe that homosexuality is quite accepted in Buddhist countries of South and Southeast Asia. This is certainly not true. In such countries, when homosexuals are thought of at all, it is more likely to be in a good-humored way or with a degree of pity. Certainly the loathing, fear and hatred that the Western homosexual has so often had to endure is absent and this is due, to a very large degree, to Buddhism's humane and tolerant influence.

A.L. De Silva,
"Homosexuality and Theravada Buddhism,"
BuddhaNet, www.buddhanet.net.

ment and become a Buddha. So when you are born as an 'in between' it must be because of bad karma, since it increases your suffering.

I still wondered why homosexuality would increase your suffering in this day and age. Surely there are lots of gay people who live enjoyable lives with plenty of material possessions, a partner they love, children they care for and the freedom to be who they really are.

"In Buddhism material wealth, physical pleasure and social status do not equal inner bliss. If gay people often are faced with intolerance, if they are kept from achieving certain liberties in life and if they struggle within themselves because of their preference, it could be considered they are not at ease and unable to find peace," he explained.

In my European mind another thought occurred. If I, especially being a straight man with Muslim roots, was to publicly announce that homosexuality led to suffering and was in fact caused by sexual misconduct, I would be considered a 'gay hater'. So could the Buddhist view on homosexuality be seen as in fact 'gay hating'?

It appears that there are no clear guidelines within the Buddhist faith concerning homosexuality.

"No, not at all. In Buddhism everyone is equal and has the same right to pursue the main goal; to purify your mind from greed, hate and delusion," the lecturer told me.

I left Somwang's office with a sense of confusion. It appears that there are no clear guidelines within the Buddhist faith concerning homosexuality. Maybe there are those who think they've discovered a lost precept, the proud owners of the Buddhist apocrypha. Or maybe the faith is open to interpretation.

At the end of the day, we might never know how Siddhartha Gautama actually thought about the matter. The scriptures were all written hundreds of years after his physical demise, but it is pretty much accepted that he was one of the greatest humanitarians that ever lived.

In Israel, Orthodox Rabbis May Allow Some Options for Homosexual Men

Anshel Pfeffer

Anshel Pfeffer is a writer and journalist who has worked as deputy managing editor of Israel's Jerusalem Post *and as a regular writer for Haaretz.com. In the following viewpoint, he reports that Orthodox Jewish rabbis in Israel traditionally would not even discuss homosexuality. However, now some Orthodox rabbis are considering allowing a gay man to have an open, nonsexual relationship with another man as long as he marries a woman and has children. Pfeffer argues that the change is important because for the first time the Orthodox Jewish faith acknowledges and tries to address the difficulties of strict Orthodox gay men.*

As you read, consider the following questions:

1. What is Atzat Nefesh, according to the author?
2. How does Rabbi Yuval Cherlow believe homosexuals should be treated?
3. What does Rabbi Burstein say about homosexuals and the closet?

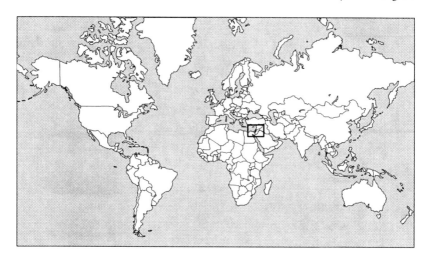

The impending halakhic [pertaining to the collective body of Jewish religious law] ruling to allow religious gay men to marry women and have children while not forcing them to keep their homosexuality a secret may seem like a rare sign of liberalism in the Orthodox [the most conservative branch of Judaism] establishment. On the other hand, it may paradoxically be a reinforcement of the wall of halakha.

Encouraging Gay Men to Have Children

The initiative was unveiled by Rabbi Menachem Burstein, head of the Jewish fertility organization Puah Institute, at a conference titled "Parenthood at Any Cost?" at the Center for Health Law and Bioethics at Ono Academic College. It is revolutionary especially in the willingness of Orthodox rabbis, including hard-liners like Rabbi Yosef Shalom Elyashiv, to even discuss such matters with the intention of actually helping a group that many rabbis are not even prepared to acknowledge even exists. The ruling, which is still under consultation, allows a religious gay man, who is committed to keeping mitzvahs [the commandments of Jewish religious law], [to] marry a woman with the understanding that he is not physically attracted to her and that whatever children they have together will be conceived either artificially or through sexual relations that will have only that target.

At the same time, that man will be allowed to maintain a relationship with his gay partner on the condition that he will not have forbidden sexual intercourse with him and will undergo counseling with therapists of Atzat Nefesh, an organization whose stated purpose is to "treat" religious gays and lesbians.

As Burstein explained to me this week [in August 2009], there are two underlying principles to the ruling. The first is that as a religious fertility institute, "we are committed to finding a solution for every part of society" and the second, regarding homosexuals is, "a rabbi cannot change the prohibition of mishkav zachar [intercourse between two males], it is from the Torah [the first five books of the Bible]. Once that is accepted, then we can look for a solution within those parameters," he said.

[A] man will be allowed to maintain a relationship with his gay partner on the condition that he will not have forbidden sexual intercourse with him.

While a number of religious couples have already married with these conditions, the official ruling has still not been given as Burstein is anxious to consult with child psychologists to hear their view on whether children can be happily raised in these circumstances.

Rabbis Disagree on Homosexuality

Things are not so clear-cut, though. There is an argument regarding the attitude towards religious homosexuals among Orthodox rabbis, mainly those belonging to the national-religious community. (Among Ashkenazi Haredi rabbis, homosexuality is a taboo subject never to be discussed publicly;

among Sephardic Haredis, it is mentioned as a disgusting sickness to be regarded with pity, at best.)[1]

More liberal-minded rabbis, like Yuval Cherlow, are willing to accept more modern psychological views that sexual orientation is not a matter of choice and maintain that everything should be done to make gay religious men and women feel welcome within their communities.

The more conservative rabbis, exemplified by Rabbi Shlomo Aviner, also preach compassion, but insist that homosexuality is a problem that can ultimately be solved by what they describe as "proper" therapy. Burstein, who on most matters is firmly in the conservative camp, is careful not to support either side in the debate.

"Having homosexual urges is not a sin," he said. "Giving in to them is. It's just like someone who has an urge to steal, as long as he fights that urge why should we blame him?"

He is also careful not to censure homosexual love, as long as it includes sexual abstinence.

"There is nothing wrong with a close and loyal friendship between two men living with each other," he said, just as long as they don't succumb to the temptation of mishkav zachar.

[Rabbi Menachem Burstein is] careful not to censure homosexual love, as long as it includes sexual abstinence.

Homosexuality Should Not Be Open

But he believes that in actuality, the number of "real" homosexuals is small. "Most men with these feelings, if they were to go for counseling with a real intention of not being homosexual, would find a way, but there are those who will always

---

1. The national-religious community refers to strict Orthodox Jews who are strong Israeli nationalists (or Zionists.) Haredi is the most theologically conservative form of Orthodox Judaism. Ashkenazi refers to Jews with roots in central and eastern Europe; Sephardic refers to Jews with roots in Spain and Portugal.

The Torah and Homosexuality

The Torah [the first five books of the Bible] does not like gays.

For some Jews, . . . the Torah may have been inspired by God, but it was written by men. Its intolerance toward homosexuals can be written off as . . . outdated bigotry. . . .

For others, . . . the Torah is the . . . word of God. Since it describes homosexuality as an "abomination," then that is how it should be treated. . . .

Then, there are the rest of us, who try to take from the best of both worlds and are faced with the challenge of reconciling the seemingly irreconcilable.

Jonathan Kamens,
"Torah Judaism, Homosexuality, and Gay Marriage,"
Jewneric *(blog), June 2, 2008. www.jewneric.com.*

remain frustrated, or not really want to take the therapy," he said. "I believe these are a small number, but we should not forsake them."

Not that he is in favor of them coming out of the closet.

"I am not telling them what to do but in my opinion, it would be better for all concerned that they didn't make a big noise about their tendencies, like going on gay parades. I say to them, remain in the closet and I will make every effort to build as large and respectable a closet as possible for you."

None of these rabbis are about to transform their views on homosexuality, but even a small change is significant.

Liberal-minded readers are certainly tut-tutting at this point at the rabbi who is intent on repressing gay people, signaling to young religious homosexuals that they have something to be ashamed of. And you don't have to be a radical gay rights activist to object to many of his views on the subject.

But he is a realist and he is also one of the few rabbis to have succeeded in receiving the tacit approval of the most senior Haredi rabbis of all streams to a series of rulings on the most sensitive subjects. None of these rabbis are about to transform their views on homosexuality, but even a small change is significant.

For many religious people, halakha is an immovable object. Certainly that is the case when it comes to prohibitions that are set out in the Torah with no room for interpretation. So what do you do if you are indeed a gay man yet believe that the act you yearn for is also an abomination before God?

Rabbi Burstein's effort will not relieve that unbearable tension, but it is at least the first open attempt by the Orthodox establishment in Israel to acknowledge its existence and find at least some ways to alleviate it.

In Israel and the United States, Conservative Synagogues Are Split over Gay Rabbis

Beth Schwartzapfel

Beth Schwartzapfel is an award-winning journalist based in Brooklyn and an adjunct lecturer in the Department of English at LaGuardia Community College. In the following viewpoint, she reports that U.S. Conservative rabbinical schools have opened their doors to gay students, but some Israeli Conservative schools have not. Since American rabbinical students often spend time studying abroad in Israel, this discrepancy has caused tension, she notes. Nonetheless, gay American Conservative rabbinical students studying in Israel have helped promote understanding, according to Schwartzapfel.

As you read, consider the following questions:

1. Which Conservative seminaries ordain gay rabbis and which do not, according to the author?
2. Who is Yonatan Gher, and why did his speaking engagement at Schechter cause controversy?
3. Why does Chesir-Teran say that it is impossible for him to move to Israel?

Beth Schwartzapfel, "Uncertain Territory: Conservative Judaism's Pioneering Gay Rabbinical Students Tread Carefully in Israel," Forward.com, December 18, 2009. Reproduced by permission of the author.

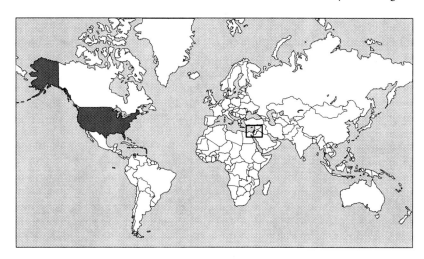

When the first openly gay rabbinic students came through the doors of Conservative Judaism's [a modern stream of Judaism that is deliberately non-fundamentalist] Jewish Theological Seminary [JTS] in 2007, there remained in the back of everyone's mind one sensitive, still-unresolved issue:

What would happen when they went to Israel?

Gay Students Face Challenges Abroad

All understood that their curriculum, like that of all JTS rabbinic students, would include a third year spent abroad at the Conservative movement's seminary in Jerusalem, which has so far refused to ordain gay rabbis.

Now, Ian Chesir-Teran and Aaron Weininger—the pioneering gay students—are poring over their Talmuds [compendiums of historical rabbinical discussions] and arguing the fine points of Jewish law at Machon Schechter in Jerusalem, JTS's sister seminary. And so far, say both the students and their school, the year abroad is proceeding smoothly, at least on the surface.

"We haven't encountered blatant homophobia," Weininger said. "And yet, there's a history there. There's that challenge of, a little bit, walking on eggshells."

This month [December 2009] marks three years since the Conservative movement's Committee on Jewish Law and Standards opened the gates for gay rabbis. Thirteen of the committee's 25 members voted for the landmark responsum, or religious position paper, advocating the move—more than twice the number of votes required to allow individual Conservative institutions to adopt the gay ordination position as their own.

The change, however, was not complete. Another responsum taking the opposite view also garnered 13 votes, leaving Conservative synagogues and schools free to adopt either position.

[December 2009] marks three years since the Conservative movement's Committee on Jewish Law and Standards opened the gates for gay rabbis.

The two American Conservative seminaries, JTS and Los Angeles's Ziegler School of Rabbinic Studies, began admitting gay students the semester immediately following the change. But the movement's two international seminaries—Machon Schechter in Jerusalem and the Seminario Rabínico Latinoamericano in Buenos Aires—declined to change their policies.

Despite this disparity, "We certainly anticipated that all of our students would continue to study in Israel, including our gay students," said Rabbi Daniel Nevins, dean of the JTS Rabbinical School. After opening enrollment to gay and lesbian students, he said, "We promptly commenced conversations with our partners in Israel and were reassured that they would welcome all of our students."

Still, some of the challenges they would face rose to the surface even during those discussions. Chesir-Teran, a former attorney who entered the seminary at the age of 36, recalled one meeting that he, Weininger and Nevins had in New York with Rabbi Einat Ramon, then dean of Machon Schechter's Rabbinical School. Upon being assured gay students would be treated equally when they came to Schechter, Chesir-Teran said he told Ramon, "I'm assuming that means we're going to be allowed to lead services and read from the Torah like everyone else." Her answer, he recalled, was, "I don't know. I have to get back to you."

Ramon later confirmed in an e-mail to Nevins that the gay students would, indeed, be allowed to do so. But the equivocation, said Chesir-Teran, was another "red flag" that made him leery about going there.

If we permit [gay marriage and ordination of gay rabbis], we should, in all intellectual fairness, permit also ... the marriage of brothers to their sisters.

Opposition to Gay Rabbis

Ramon's public pronouncements against gay ordination also stoked the two students' concerns. In a *Washington Jewish Week* opinion piece shortly after the committee's historic vote, Ramon, explaining her opposition to the change, avowed, "Judaism has always been clear and unambivalent toward the centrality of the heterosexual family." And in a September 2007 policy statement, Ramon wrote, "If we permit [gay marriage and ordination of gay rabbis], we should, in all intellectual fairness, permit also all other forms of prohibited sexual activity and allow the marriage of brothers to their sisters."

Ramon, who still teaches at Schechter, left her position as dean this past September [2009]. And though no one claims the move was connected to her pronouncements on gay ordination, supporters of the historic change say Ramon's departure has eased the atmosphere for gay and lesbian students at Schechter considerably.

Ramon declined to comment for this [viewpoint]. "I have written and said what I had to say," she told the *Forward.*

Nevertheless, during her tenure, the relationship between the two schools was sometimes strained. For example, Schechter put its foot down in March 2008, when several JTS students studying there sought to mark the one-year anniversary of the change in JTS's admissions policy. The students invited Yonatan Gher, then the incoming director of the gay community center Jerusalem Open House, to speak about his experience as a gay man in the Israeli Conservative movement. But after a dispute with Ramon and others in the administration, the students were forced to hold the event off campus.

Nevins cringed when asked about this event. "That was an incident where no one was at their best," he acknowledged. "It was a very painful moment."

Heading into their year abroad with this history in mind, Chesir-Teran, Weininger, and several other students lobbied the JTS administration for alternatives to Machon Schechter.

"The very thought, frankly, of being told by my home institution that I have to study at a school that wouldn't ordain me, that wouldn't confer on me the title of 'rabbi,' is very challenging," Chesir-Teran said.

But one option JTS never considered was allowing the students to study at another school. This is a route the Ziegler School took when it announced in January that it would end its 10-year relationship with Machon Schechter. The shift, says Ziegler dean Rabbi Bradley Artson, is unrelated to Schechter's stand on gay ordination. But Ziegler now sends its students to the Conservative Yeshiva, a co-educational, egalitarian school for Diaspora Jews in Jerusalem.

JTS, said Nevins, is committed to sending its students to an Israeli institution, where they can take classes, taught in Hebrew, alongside Israelis. "The other options out there were American environments, not Israeli environments," he said.

Efforts at Reconciliation

Though Schechter's policy against gay ordination continues, the two rabbis selected to fill Ramon's position this past July are seen as friendly toward the cause of gay students. Rabbi Moshe Silberschein, appointed dean, was ordained at JTS in 1981 and taught for many years at the Reform [a Jewish movement friendly to modernization]-affiliated Hebrew Union College in Jerusalem, which has admitted gay students since 1990. Rabbi Tamar Elad-Appelbaum, appointed associate dean, is a member of Keshet, the Conservative group pushing for gay inclusion.

Rabbinical students say that simply being who they are and telling their personal stories has had a profound impact on many of their teachers and fellow students.

Among their reasons for taking their new positions, said Silberschein, is a desire "to unite the movement."

"I'd like to think that we're bringing a new spirit of conciliation," he said. "As far as I'm concerned, it's a new page."

Nevertheless, Silberschein says, the school's ordination policy is unlikely to change anytime soon. While Ramon was dean, she also served as Schechter's *posek*, or *halachic* [pertaining to Jewish law] decision maker. When she stepped down, the two positions were split, and Rabbi David Golinkin was appointed *posek*. Golinkin decided that Schechter would continue to abide by the more conservative responsum. And Silberschein, whatever his personal views, defers to Golinkin. "I took this job knowing clearly that Rabbi Golinkin is the *posek* for Schechter," he said. "But I wanted to once again build bridges with the movement and Schechter and the movement with JTS."

Now that they've settled into their time in Jerusalem, both Weininger and Chesir-Teran are taking stock.

"Having lived now in Jerusalem for almost four months, and really having adjusted well with my husband and three kids here, we've indulged a little bit in fantasies about what it would be like to make *aliyah*, to move to Israel, and to make a home for ourselves here," said Chesir-Teran. "But I know that that's really impossible, because I couldn't continue my studies at Machon Schechter."

That said, "having a place at the table is a blessing and a privilege," he said.

Both rabbinical students say that simply being who they are and telling their personal stories has had a profound impact on many of their teachers and fellow students. Being at JTS and at Schechter, said Chesir-Teran, has meant "having opportunities to interact on a daily basis with future rabbis, and to let them see how I live my life, just as I see how they live their lives—to show that my life is equally as holy and equally as mundane as their lives."

Islam Is Morally Conflicted About Homosexuality

TheReligionofPeace.com

TheReligionofPeace.com is a nonpartisan website concerned with Islam's true political and cultural teachings according to its own texts. The following viewpoint argues that Islamic teachings, including the Qur'an, other important texts, and the policies of modern Islamic states, are strongly opposed to homosexuality. At the same time, the viewpoint notes, there are passages in the Qur'an and incidents in Islamic history that present homosexuality in a neutral or positive light. The viewpoint concludes that Islam's moral attitude toward homosexuality is confused.

As you read, consider the following questions:

1. According to the viewpoint, what language in the Qur'an has led Islamic scholars to argue that homosexuals should be stoned?

2. What was the *jizya*?

3. In which two Islamic countries does the viewpoint say that homosexuals face the death penalty?

What is Islam's position on homosexuality?

Islamic law teaches that homosexuality is a vile form of fornication, punishable by death. Beneath the surface, however, there are implied references to homosexual behavior in paradise, and it has been a part of historical Arab and Muslim culture.

The Qur'an on Homosexuality

Qur'an [the Islamic holy text]—"*. . . For ye practice your lusts on men in preference to women: ye are indeed a people transgressing beyond bounds. . . . And we rained down on them a shower (of brimstone)*"—An account that is borrowed from the Biblical story of Sodom [in which God destroys the sinful towns of Sodom and Gomorrah]. Muslim scholars through the centuries have interpreted the "rain of stones" on the town as meaning that homosexuals should be stoned, since no other reason is given for the people's destruction.

Qur'an—"*Will ye commit abomination such as no creature ever did before you?*" This verse is part of the previous text and it establishes . . . homosexuality as different from (and much worse than) adultery or other sexual sin. According to the Arabic grammar, homosexuality is called *the* worst sin, while references elsewhere describe other forms of nonmarital sex as being "among great sins."

Qur'an—"*Of all the creatures in the world, will ye approach males, And leave those whom Allah has created for you to be your mates? Nay, ye are a people transgressing.*"

[The Qur'an] establishes . . . homosexuality as different from (and much worse than) adultery or other sexual sin.

Qur'an—"*If two men among you are guilty of lewdness, punish them both. If they repent and amend, Leave them alone.*"

Interestingly, the same rules don't apply in paradise, where martyrs for the cause of Allah [the Muslim name for God] enjoy an orgy of virgins and "*perpetual youth*" (otherwise

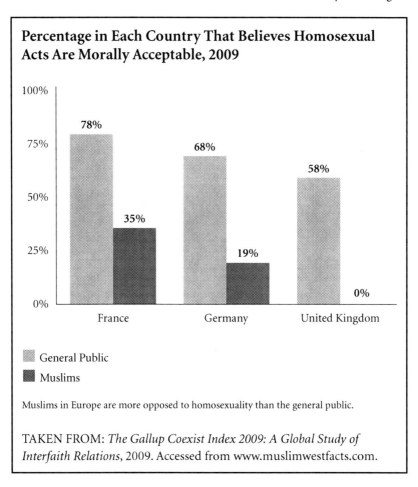

Percentage in Each Country That Believes Homosexual Acts Are Morally Acceptable, 2009

Muslims in Europe are more opposed to homosexuality than the general public.

TAKEN FROM: *The Gallup Coexist Index 2009: A Global Study of Interfaith Relations*, 2009. Accessed from www.muslimwestfacts.com.

known as "*boys.*") Qur'an bluntly states, "*And immortal boys will circulate among them, when you see them you will count them as scattered pearls.*" Technically, the mere presence of boys doesn't necessarily mean sex, however it is strongly implied from the particular emphasis on the effeminacy, handsomeness and "freshness" of the boys. The female virgins of paradise are also compared to pearls.

[Website editor's note: We are *not* implying a link between homosexuality and pedophilia here anymore than we are implying one between heterosexuality and pedophilia when mentioning that Muhammad's preferred wife was a 9-year-old.]

The Hadith on Homosexuality

There are several lesser hadith [narrations concerning the words and deeds of Muhammad] stating, "if a man comes upon a man, then they are both adulterers," "If a woman comes upon a woman, they are both adulteresses," "When a man mounts another man, the throne of God shakes," and "Kill the one that is doing it and also kill the one that it is being done to."

Abu Dawud—"The Messenger of Allaah (peace and blessings of Allaah be upon him) said, 'Whoever you find doing the action of the people of Loot [that is engaging in homosexuality], execute the one who does it and the one to whom it is done.'"

Abu Dawud—"If a man who is not married is seized committing sodomy [performing anal sex], he will be stoned to death." (Note that sodomizing one's wife is implicitly approved).

When a man mounts another man, the throne of God shakes.

Bukhari—"The Prophet cursed effeminate men, those men who are in the similitude (assume the manners of women), and those women who assume the manners of men, and he said, 'Turn them out of your houses.' The Prophet turned out such-and-such man, and Umar turned out such-and-such woman."

al-Tirmidhi, Sunan—[Muhammad said] "Whoever is found conducting himself in the manner of the people of Lot, [that is, behaving as homosexuals] kill the doer and the receiver."

Reliance of the Traveller—"May Allah curse him who does what Lot's people did." This is also repeated in three other places.

Homosexuality in Muslim History

When Mehmed conquered Constantinople in 1453, the Muslim general demanded the 14-year-old son of one of the city's

Christian leaders as his sexual concubine (the father and son chose death instead). Subsequent Ottoman administrators also engaged in homosexuality, often with the boys of conquered populations who could not afford to satisfy the *jizya* (poll tax on non-Muslims) in any other way than to relinquish their own children to the Religion of Peace.

And yet, homosexuals have been beheaded, hung and stoned in modern Saudi Arabia and Iran, where Muhammad's laws are applied most strictly. Five other Muslim countries also have the death penalty on their books for homosexual behavior. In the past, gays were burned as well. As one cleric recently put it, the only point of theological debate is over *how* the offender should be killed.

The only point of theological debate is over how *the offender should be killed.*

Thus illustrates the moral confusion that Islam has with homosexuality. There are several places in the Qur'an where the story of Sodom is repeated, with emphasis placed on the destruction of the town for homosexual lewdness. Also, according to [political scientist and historian] Serge Trifkovic:

> Mohammed's first successor Abu Bakr reportedly had a homosexual burned at the stake. The fourth caliph, Mohammed's son-in-law Ali, ordered a sodomite thrown from the minaret of a mosque. Others he ordered to be stoned. One of the earliest and most authoritative commentators on the Koran, Ibn Abbas (died 687) blended both approaches into a two-step execution in which "the sodomite should be thrown from the highest building in the town and then stoned."

Although some Muslim political leaders in the West join with social liberals in alliances that occasionally include residual support for gay rights and civil unions, this appears to be more a matter of expediency than genuine concern. There has never been any noticeable effort on the part of Muslim leaders in the West to relieve the plight of homosexuals in Islamic countries overseas—where their influence would surely carry more weight than that of their secular allies.

The Russian Orthodox Church Is Opposed to Homosexuality

Spiegel in an interview with Metropolitan Kyrill

Metropolitan Kyrill is the foreign minister of the Russian Ortho-dox Church; Spiegel *is a German weekly magazine. In the fol-lowing interview, Kyrill explains to* Spiegel *that the Russian Or-thodox Church holds homosexuality to be a sin. Kyrill adds that gay people should not be persecuted, but neither, he argues, should homosexuality be promoted. Otherwise, he concludes, morality becomes relative, which is disastrous.*

As you read, consider the following questions:

1. What percentage of Russians call themselves Orthodox Christians and what percentage attend church regularly, according to Metropolitan Kyrill?
2. According to Metropolitan Kyrill, the Communists said that good was what was good for whom, and what was the result?
3. What does Metropolitan Kyrill say is the difference be-tween men and animals?

*S*piegel: *It's clear to see that many Russians have adopted a liberal Western lifestyle. Sex before marriage is normal for many people, and only a small minority attends church services regularly. How firmly established are Christian values in Russia?*

Spiegel Online, "Interview with Russian Orthodox Metropolitan Kyrill: 'The Bible Calls It a Sin,'" *Spiegel Online*, January 10, 2008. Copyright © 2008 *Spiegel Online*. Repro-duced by permission.

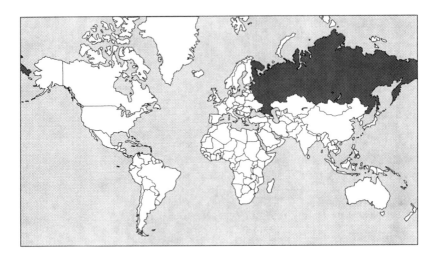

Spirituality and the Liberal West

[Metropolitan] Kyrill: Spirituality can't be measured with statistics. Nevertheless, we aren't afraid of comparisons. Less than 20 years after the fall of the Soviet Union [which opposed religious observance, and which fell in 1991], the number of churches has quadrupled, we now have twice as many dioceses, and the number of monasteries has grown by a factor of 32—to 700—today. Fifteen thousand young people are studying theology. On the other hand, even though 80 percent of newborns are baptized in Russia, only 60 percent of Russians call themselves Orthodox Christians, and less than 10 percent attend church regularly—even fewer in some provinces. In other words, we don't have to build any new churches, but what we must do is help our people understand how important it is to adhere to Christian values. Whether we succeed also depends on whether we can rid ourselves of outside influences.

You are referring to the liberal West. What troubles you, for example, about homosexuals marching through the streets of Moscow in a parade, just as they do in Berlin or Amsterdam?

It distorts the boundary between good and evil, between sin and sanctity. Even adultery is apparently no longer considered a sin, and despite the fact that every adulterer senses that he has done something wrong. But human beings have a conscience. That's something even the Marxists were unable to eliminate. They had an explanation for everything, a self-contained philosophy in which being determined consciousness—just as your philosophers in Germany say, the conscience is the result of cultural development. But whether you are in Papua New Guinea, Munich or Novosibirsk in Siberia, the principles are the same everywhere: Thou shall not steal, though shall not kill. . . .

. . . but not everyone says: Thou shall not be gay. Why should people have to conceal their homosexuality?

Even adultery is apparently no longer considered a sin, despite the fact that every adulterer senses that he has done something wrong.

Do Not Propagate Sin

The Bible calls it a sin. But we do not condemn these people. The church is opposed to these people being persecuted or offended. But why should sin be propagated? The gay parade is a blatant display of sodomy [anal sex]. In that case, we might as well promote other sins, as has long been the case on television. This degenerates public morality. It is the church's job to call a sin a sin. Otherwise it no longer serves a purpose. Unfortunately, the tendency in today's world is to champion the freedom of choice, while freedom from evil is virtually forgotten.

It's human for a person to be homosexual. How can something that is human be a sin?

And what, in your opinion, is adultery—something good or something bad?

This decision lies within the conscience of every individual. We aren't talking about just any decision. We are talking about morals. They want us to believe that morality is relative. But that's completely untrue. The Communists said that good is what is good for the working class. That was relative morality—and 60 million people were exterminated. Hitler claimed that what is good is what is good for greater Germany. That too cost millions of lives. Morality is either absolute or it doesn't exist at all. If you can justify homosexuality, why not pedophilia?

The gay parade is a blatant display of sodomy. In that case, we might as well promote other sins, as has long been the case on television. . . . It is the church's job to call a sin a sin.

But that's an enormous difference! Sexuality relates to adults who can decide for themselves. Pedophilia involves children being abused and has nothing to do with human freedom.

In a few years, they'll tell you that 12-year-old girls used to be children, but that they are now much further developed. Twenty years ago, no one would have dreamed that Germany would pass a law one day that recognizes homosexual marriages. But now that too has been accepted. We are talking about preserving the principle. There is something we call a general moral nature.

And it depends on time and region. There are ethnic groups that allow polygamy, for instance.

[Russian author Fyodor] Dostoyevsky wrote that God and the devil are fighting for control in the heart of man. Nowadays many pursue the logic that everything they want ought to be good and justified. We are too quick to treat emotions that ultimately harm us as natural needs. When moral foundations are shaken, we unleash our instincts. But released instincts belong in the animal world. What I am saying is something that the liberal *Spiegel* will never print: You undoubtedly think that this Metropolitan Kyrill is out of his mind and that what he is saying is complete nonsense.

We like to argue. But you can't possibly characterize homosexuality as an animal instinct?

Instinct is not a term with negative connotations. Take hunger, thirst, the sex drive, for example. If God had not given us these instincts, man would not exist. The difference between men and animals is that men can control their drives.

Catholic Spirituality Can Embrace Homosexuality

Sebastian Moore

Sebastian Moore is a theologian, poet, Benedictine monk, and author of The Contagion of Jesus: Doing Theology as if It Mattered. *In the following viewpoint, Moore argues that the Catholic Church has a tradition of same-sex friendships and an understanding of sexual love, both of which can be of spiritual help to homosexuals as the taboo against same-sex relationships dissolves. In addition, Moore notes that homosexuality is most accepted in the parts of the world that are Christian, and he argues that this is because Christianity is the religion that is the fullest revelation of God.*

As you read, consider the following questions:

1. According to Moore, what is the controlling principle of the norms in the gay and lesbian world?

2. Moore says that the Lutheran tradition equates original sin with what?

3. What part of Africa is tolerant of homosexuality, and why does Moore say that this is so?

The Anglican Communion appears to be in its death-throes over homosexuality. [Editor's note: The Anglican Church has been pulled between those who support gay marriage and

Sebastian Moore, "An Irrepressible Reflection," sebastianmoore.blogspot.com, November 15, 2007. Reproduced by permission.

ordination of gay priests and those who oppose both.] With a confidence that now astounds us, the antigay members are setting up large bodies of ecclesially legitimized dissent. Theologies are erected against each other.

Homophobia Collapses

And, all the time, inexorably, elementally, the homosexual taboo collapses. Nothing can reverse this collapse, since it is the prevailing of love and tolerance over all that bias can erect against it. Nothing can reverse this collapse, which is freeing a sizable worldwide minority from a self-hatred that society imposes and the Holy Spirit opposes. Nothing can reverse this collapse, which puts an end to needless suffering on an enormous scale. Theologies demanding the taboo must fall like a house of cards.

And with a wonderful irony, the Catholic Church, that bases its moral teaching not ultimately on scripture but on the Natural Law [a law set by nature, which is valid everywhere] which expresses the best insights we have from our sciences into the good life, is in a position to ask what all the fuss is about.

Nothing can reverse this collapse [of the homosexual taboo], since it is the prevailing of love and tolerance over all that bias can erect against it.

Still, the effect of the collapse has further implications, as follows. The effect of the taboo, which implies the non-existence societally of gays and lesbians, is that there is no legislation for them, meaning by 'legislation' here simply recognized customs. Thus when the taboo collapses, they find themselves in a world without moral landmarks, with promiscuity the norm. So, the collapse of the taboo requires a humane filling-in with moral norms comparable to those that

---

The Taboo Against Homosexuality Is Decreasing in the United Kingdom

Year	Percentage Who Believe Homosexuality Is Wrong
1983	62%
2008	36%

TAKEN FROM: Jessica Green, "Social Attitudes Survey Finds Far Greater Acceptance of Homosexuality," *Pink News*, January 26, 2010. www.pinknews.co.uk.

---

are present in the straight world. These norms already exist, of course, in the gay and lesbian world, and the controlling principle is friendship and fidelity.

As the taboo ceases to exist, these norms will assume a crucial importance. And as the Catholic Church, the most sexually conservative of Christian bodies, adjusts to the collapse of the taboo, its teachers will find available a long tradition of church-blessed friendships which were not specified as sexual. . . .

It goes without saying that serious gay and lesbian people do not regard promiscuity as an option. They are human beings, and humans make friends and friendship makes demands. The assumption that were the church to accept homosexuality as a valid orientation the result would be a Catholic homosexual mayhem is insulting to gays and lesbians.

The tradition of church-blessed friendships is Catholic, it belongs to the world of Christendom, and this fact is an extension of the irony pointed out earlier in this [viewpoint]. The surprising richness of the Catholic tradition in the moral area that has been under the reign of the taboo, so that when the taboo loses its hold, the Catholic tradition has much to fall back on, is one of the joys of that tradition. . . .

Christianity Is Tied to the Rejection of Homophobia

Now the collapse of the taboo is culturally selective. Broadly speaking, it is happening in the Christian world, in the world that has been crucially influenced by faith in Jesus, who brought us freedom and bought it for us on a cross.

Not surprisingly, it is where the taboo is collapsing that governments are instituting the so-called civil partnerships. This enactment, far from signalling a decay in public morals, shows an awareness of the moral dimension of the collapse of the taboo. And difficult as it may be to accept this, this new legislation expresses a moral maturity well in advance of the still official teaching of the [Catholic] church, for which homosexuality is 'a disorder'—a teaching, incidentally, that goes against the Council of Trent [a sixteenth-century conference that defined many Catholic teachings] on the nature of original sin and of our redemption from it, which rejects the Lutheran notion that equates original sin with 'concupiscence' [or sexual desire], so that you could have an inherited depraved desire, which the 'disorder' of homosexuality could be taken to exemplify.

This coincidence of the demise of the taboo with Christian regions of humanity is not surprising if we believe that Jesus brings a fuller revelation of God than do the other avatars of humanity.

In sum. Two most bewilderingly opposed moral positions on homosexuality depend on whether you are, or are not, experiencing the collapse of the taboo. Nothing is easier to understand than homophobia. It is natural where the collapse is not an established societal fact; it collapses as the taboo collapses. Dr Rowan Williams [the Anglican Archbishop of Canterbury] and a Latvian cardinal whose name escapes me are both Christian prelates. But the former inhabits the collapse, the latter the taboo in force, so that he can declare civil partnerships to be more insidious than Soviet communism, whose dominance [in] his own country endured for forty years. He said that civil partnerships expressed 'sexual atheism.'

Some time ago, the *Guardian* carried a two-page map of the world, on which were shown the areas where the taboo is finished and the areas still under its control. Broadly speaking, the tolerant areas are Christian or post-Christian. Strikingly, most of Africa is intolerant, some states having the death penalty for homosexuals, whereas Capetown [South Africa] is tolerant; for Capetown has seen the Christian battle for civil rights versus apartheid, associated with the noble memory of Bishop Trevor Huddleston [an Anglican priest famous for antiapartheid activism]. It is not ecumenically fashionable to point out that this coincidence of the demise of the taboo with Christian regions of humanity is not surprising if we believe that Jesus brings a fuller revelation of God than do the other avatars of humanity.

The Catholic Church Rejects Homosexuality

Courage

Courage is an apostolate of the Roman Catholic Church that ministers to those with same-sex attractions and their loved ones. In the following viewpoint, the organization says that the Catholic Church condemns homosexual acts as damaging, sinful, and against the design of God. However, the viewpoint argues that the church has no prejudice against those who commit homosexual acts and condemns discrimination against homosexuals. The viewpoint concludes that abandoning the homosexual life for Catholicism and chastity can bring peace and happiness.

As you read, consider the following questions:

1. According to Courage, why did God create sex?
2. Why does the viewpoint say that the Catholic Church refuses to call anyone a homosexual?
3. What four factors does Courage say are necessary for someone to leave the homosexual life?

You sometimes hear: "The [Catholic] Church accepts homosexuality as natural and normal," or "The Church condemns homosexuals." To clear up that confusion, this [viewpoint] will quote and comment on eleven statements from a 1986 CDF [Congregation for the Doctrine of the Faith, which

Courage, "Living in Truth: Eleven Church Teachings on Homosexuality," 2000–2009. Reproduced by permission.

oversees Catholic doctrine] letter entitled, "Letter to the Bishops of the Catholic Church on the Pastoral Care of Homosexual Persons."

Married Love and Children

1. Loving and Life-Giving Union.

> The Church . . . celebrates the divine plan of the loving and life-giving union of men and women in the sacrament of marriage.

God created sex for two combined purposes: the happiness of a man and woman uniting in married love, and the happiness of new life being born from that union. Take away either one—for instance with adultery, prostitution, masturbation, premarital sex, or homogenital activity—and sexual activity turns negative and limiting, because those two purposes are built into us. We are made physically for loving and for generating new life. Sexual acts which are anything less than that will separate us from part of ourselves and from what God wants for us; they leave out and suppress part of what sex is and part of who we are.

2. A Complementary Sexual Design.

> To choose someone of the same sex for one's sexual activity is to annul [erase] the rich symbolism and meaning, not to mention the goals, of the Creator's sexual design. Homosexual activity is not a complementary union able to transmit life. . . .

God's plan for us is to engage the mystery of male and female, travel the distance between the sexes, and unite. Homosexuality uses sex for something other than what the Creator intended. The nature of our bodies requires no elaborate scientific data to prove the obvious fact that our bodies are not made for same-sex union. The Church is saying our hearts aren't either, and so it's not good for us or for our long-term happiness and growth. God created us physically and emotionally for "complementary union" and procreation.

Homosexuality uses sex for something other than what the Creator intended.

Against Morality

3. The Homosexual Inclination Is Objectively Disordered.

Although the particular inclination of the homosexual person is not a sin, it is a more or less strong tendency toward an intrinsic moral evil; and thus the inclination itself must be seen as an objective disorder.

Homosexual erotic attractions may arise for a number of reasons which can be understood, both psychologically and emotionally. Sometimes they're temporary—especially for adolescents—but for some people, homosexual feelings are deep-rooted and difficult to overcome. The Church says it's not a sin to have such attractions (especially if the erotic element is not willfully cultivated), but it is an objective disorder, a problem.

It can be difficult to understand what an "objective disorder" is. It means that the very inclination toward a same-sex act indicates that the desire itself is moving in the wrong direction; ordinarily the vast majority of men and women have a natural God-given attraction toward physical union with a person of the opposite sex. This is natural and good because it leads the majority of people into marriage whereas same-sex attractions while not sinful, end up in a disordered act if one gives into them.

It may be objected that a man lusting for a woman is a disordered act, but the inclination to such an act is considered natural but misdirected under ordinary circumstances. Under the circumstance of marriage, however, this inclination is good because it leads to a strengthening of the union between a man and woman and the procreation of a child.

Same-sex erotic attractions do not lead to a strengthening of the union between a man and woman nor to the procreation of a child; therefore, they are considered objectively disordered but not sinful in and of themselves.

4. Not Morally Acceptable.

Therefore special concern and pastoral attention should be directed toward those who have this condition, lest they be led to believe that the living out of this orientation in homosexual activity is a morally acceptable option. It is not. . . . It is only in the marital relationship that the use of the sexual faculty can be morally good.

The very inclination toward a same-sex act indicates that the desire itself is moving in the wrong direction.

The only reason the Church goes to the trouble of calling certain activities morally wrong is that those activities cause real harm. To act on homosexual feelings is to increase their strength. Many who were formerly active in the homosexual lifestyle report that the temporary sexual pleasure—and this is true of every form of unhealthy sex—left them profoundly empty. On the other hand, when they abstained from illicit sexual activity, even if abstaining was a struggle, they found they experienced greater peace and confidence.

Catholicism Is Not Prejudiced Against Homosexuals

5. The Church Calls No One "A Homosexual."

Today, the Church . . . refuses to consider the person as a "heterosexual" or a "homosexual," and insists that every person has a fundamental identity: the creature of God, and by grace, His child and heir to eternal life.

The Church won't put a label on anyone. To say someone is "gay" or "lesbian" or a "homosexual" is to define a whole person by just one aspect. It can lock up a person's identity and block further emotional growth. That's just the sort of labeling which gives rise to prejudice and discrimination. The Church stands against any behavior it calls immoral, but always teaches support and respect for the person. Labeling limits and disrespects people.

People with homosexual struggles face many challenges.
They need love and encouragement, not mistreatment.

---

6. The Church Condemns Violent Malice.

It is deplorable that homosexual persons have been and are the object of violent malice in speech or in action. Such treatment deserves condemnation from the Church's pastors wherever it occurs.

Some people despise those who struggle with homosexual attractions. The Church condemns any expressions of that attitude, for "instance": anti-gay or anti-lesbian jokes, verbal and physical attack, social exclusion, rejection of friends or family members, avoidance of the topic of homosexuality, and so on. That behavior is all very wrong. It's what the Church calls "a sin against charity." People with homosexual struggles face many challenges. They need love and encouragement, not mistreatment.

7. Respect Each Person.

The intrinsic dignity of each person must always be respected in word, in action, and in law.

When you hear insulting remarks about people who struggle with homosexuality, the Church is saying: Don't stand for it. Speak up. And when a friend or family member confides in you about experiencing homosexual attractions, that's

---

Homosexual Acts Do Not Define People

Homosexual acts *are* depraved, but that's not the same as saying that homosexuals are depraved. The [Catholic] Church, basing itself on human reason, says that in moral questions we must distinguish between the act and the person committing the act. Homosexuals have the same intrinsic dignity as all other human beings. Christ died for them as much as for you and me, and God loves them no less.

Kenneth J. Howell,
"Does the Catholic Church Condemn Homosexuals?"
This Rock, July–August 2004. www.catholic.com.

---

the moment your friendship and Christian response really count. Good friends also challenge one another, so you can and should say what you believe. You can continue to show both Christian love *and* faithfulness to the Truth, no matter what decision they make.

The Church Must Speak the Truth

8. Pressure on the Church.

> . . . increasing numbers of people today, even within the Church, are bringing enormous pressure to bear on the Church to accept the homosexual condition as though it were not disordered and to condone homosexual activity.

One of the Church's toughest duties is to speak the truth with love and confront the self-destructive ideas and behavior of any society, and often those societies resist. Our Christian "tough love" insists that God intends more for us than homosexual activity can ever offer. Our long-standing Judeo-Christian tradition is coming under strong attack especially in America. Every young Catholic can expect to feel this pressure—some of it even from dissenters within the Church, some of it from otherwise respected teachers or counselors. If you openly affirm the Church's teaching and ask your friend to question the "gay-positive" path, you will very likely get labeled "homophobic." It takes courage to speak an unpopular truth, but it's an act of real love. Reaffirm your love to your friend and hold your ground.

9. *Generous and Giving People.*

> Homosexual activity . . . thwarts the call to a life of that form of self-giving which the Gospel says is the essence of Christian living. This does not mean that homosexual persons are not often generous and giving of themselves; but when they engage in homosexual activity they confirm within themselves a disordered sexual inclination which is essentially self-indulgent.

What if your actively homosexual friends are otherwise good people? Their sexual activity still works against that goodness, and for friendship's sake and honesty's sake you need to say clearly, at least once, what you believe and why. Apart from that, you can still affirm other good things you see in your friend, as the Church does. And you can still be there for your friend no matter what, and say so. Such loyalty has at times been the lifeline for people who deep down didn't want the homosexual identity and life but had been convinced they had no choice in the matter—because they'd never heard anyone say anything different.

10. *Always and Totally Compulsive?*

> What is at all costs to be avoided is the unfounded and demeaning assumption that the sexual behavior of homosexual persons is always and totally compulsive and therefore inculpable.

"I can't stop" is the cry of the addict, and it means a person feels that his/her freedom has been taken over by something else. But not all homosexuality is compulsive, especially at first. Some people experiment with homosexual sex just to see if they like it. Sex just for pleasure, however, often leads to sexual addiction—whether it's heterosexual or homosexual. Catholic teaching reminds us that our free will is God's gift, and anything that controls us is against God's purposes. Some people who were once actively homosexual testify that it didn't take long to become deeply addicted to gay or lesbian sex. Overcoming the addiction was a very difficult, but not impossible, struggle.

One of the Church's toughest duties is to speak the truth with love and confront the self-destructive ideas and behavior of any society.

---

11. Abandoning Homosexuality.

Abandonment of homosexual activity will require a profound collaboration of the individual with God's liberating grace.

Many people experience difficulty in trying to leave the terribly risky homosexual life. Four factors are necessary for success: deep conviction that only chaste living is good, sturdy support from others, total personal effort, and reliance on God. Many people do successfully establish a life of sexual self-control. But are they happy? Popular opinion says, "No!" imagining a never-ending torment of suppressed desire. Not so, say these over-comers. They report instead great happiness and much gratitude to God for being set free at last from the demeaning power of their lust. The result is increased self-confidence and inner peace.

In Nigeria, Anglicans Support Imprisonment for Homosexuality

Faith J.H. Mcdonnell

Faith J.H. Mcdonnell directs the Institute on Religion & Democracy's Religious Liberty program and Church Alliance for a New Sudan, and she is the author of Girl Soldier: A Story of Hope for Northern Uganda's Children. *In the following viewpoint, she responds to a* New York Times *article about the archbishop of the Anglican Church of Nigeria, Peter J. Akinola. Mcdonnell argues that the* New York Times *article portrays Akinola and the Nigerian Anglican Communion in terms of a pro-gay/anti-gay issue, but the real reason for the views expressed by Akinola and his parishioners is a belief in the biblical view of sin and the place of Jesus. Mcdonnell provides further context for the debate by mentioning that homosexuality has been illegal in Nigeria for years and that there is pressure from the Nigerian Muslim communities to impose the death penalty for homosexuality.*

As you read, consider the following questions:

1. How many Anglican dioceses were there in Nigeria in 1998, and how may were there at the time of writing?

Faith J.H. Mcdonnell, "Out of Africa," *The American Spectator*, January 11, 2007. Reproduced by permission.

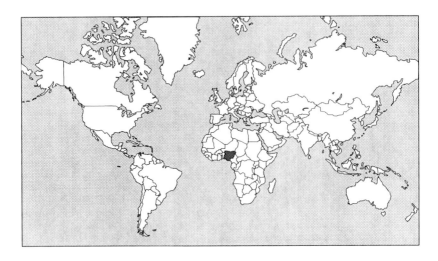

2. Why does McDonnell call Ian Douglas's portrayal of Akinola as a "spokesperson for a new Anglicanism" disingenuous?

3. What does Akinola write to the CANA churches in the United States about the true position of the Nigerian Anglican churches?

As the Episcopal Church begins to shed parishes like a dried-up Christmas tree sheds needles, it must have been comforting to the denomination to receive a sizeable Christmas present from the *New York Times*.

What could more clearly say "Merry Christmas" to the denizens of 815 Second Avenue, the church's national center, than the total trashing of the Archbishop of the Anglican Church of Nigeria, Peter J. Akinola, on the front page of the newspaper's Christmas Day edition?

With the headline "At Axis of Episcopal Split, an Anti-Gay Nigerian," the *Times* story spins the crisis in the Anglican Communion as a simple pro-gay/anti-gay issue. But it wasn't just differing views of homosexuality that led nine parishes in the Episcopal Church's Diocese of Virginia to affiliate with the

Province of Nigeria. And it wasn't just an "anti-gay bishop" that brought about the Convocation of Anglicans in North America (CANA).

The root cause the *Times* ignores is a theological one concerning differences over many tenets of the faith: the nature of sin; the authority of Scripture; whether Jesus is the only way to God; whether God is a Father, or as the new Presiding Bishop of the Episcopal Church would have us believe, a Mother. The *Times* portrayal is guaranteed to make the Nigerian church and American traditionalists appear ignorant and hateful.

That's why the paper seems alarmed by the size of Akinola's flock—there are more than 17 million members of the Anglican Church of Nigeria. (Think of the potential number of homophobes being indoctrinated!) And whereas the *Times'* pet Episcopal Church is diminishing more with each passing year, the Nigerian province continues to grow in spite of persecution. In 1998, there were 61 dioceses, and today there are 78—many of the new ones formed in the Muslim-dominated northern and middle "belt" areas of the country.

The root cause the Times *ignores is a theological one concerning differences over many tenets of the faith. . . .*

The *Times* reinforces its "anti-gay Nigerian" theme with an introductory story about the archbishop's "first and only time" to knowingly shake a gay person's hand. Akinola recounts how while in mid-handshake with a man in New York, the man introduced him to his "partner of many years" while shaking his head in what the reporter describes as "wonder and horror." "I said, 'Oh!'" he told the *Times.* "I jumped back."

Akinola may have been shaking his head with dismay over a province of the Anglican Communion where same-sex partners are not just accepted but exalted. And perhaps the archbishop jumped back because he is savvier to Episcopal Church operatives than for which he was given credit. African bishops and clergy from Sudan and Uganda, for example, had been introduced to the same gay man and his partner while the Episcopal News Service conveniently happened to be close by. They seized the moment on camera to exploit those Africans—either for shaking hands or for not shaking hands. Maybe Akinola did not want to join the ranks of those who had been used by the Episcopal Church to provide credibility for itself in the wider Communion.

The rest of the article continues in this vein. Akinola is called "the most visible advocate for a literal interpretation of Scripture," which supposedly challenges the "traditional Anglican approach of embracing diverse theological viewpoints." The archbishop is further identified as "the 62-year-old son of an illiterate widow." The reference to his mother's lack of education—not uncommon among African women of the time or even today—seems to suggest that only the ignorant and uneducated have this perspective on the Bible.

Yet the reporters admit that Akinola's views on sexual morality fit the Nigerian mainstream. "Attitudes towards homosexuality, women's rights, and marriage are dictated largely by scripture and enforced by deep social taboos," the *Times* scolds. These attitudes contrast sharply with those inculcated by some American church activists, who make use of transgendered sock puppets to promote "Queer Week" at Episcopal Divinity School (EDS) in Massachusetts.

Maybe the *Times* should have interviewed the sock puppet rather than EDS Professor Ian Douglas. Douglas says Akinola "sees himself as the spokesperson for a new Anglicanism, and thus is a direct challenge to the historic authority of the Archbishop of Canterbury." But Douglas's concern for "historic authority" seems disingenuous. He was present at General Convention 2003 during debates over the consecration of Gene Robinson as bishop of New Hampshire. Those in favor of Robinson justified their challenge to historic authority by invoking the Holy Spirit (in favor of consecrating as bishop a man who had left his wife and children to live in a homosexual relationship). Falsely portraying orthodox, traditional faith as "new" Anglicanism is part of the spin.

In a parting thrust, the *Times* expounds upon proposed Nigerian legislation that would make any public expression of homosexuality a crime punishable by five years' imprisonment. What the story fails to mention is that homosexual activity has actually been illegal in Nigeria, as in many African countries, for years. According to Article 214 of the Nigerian Penal Code, sanctions include up to 14 years imprisonment. But recently, homosexual activism sponsored by organizations from outside of the country has enflamed the already-heightened religious tensions. Islamists seek to reform the country by imposing a legal code that calls for the *stoning* of homosexuals. In response, Nigerian President [Olusegun] Obasanjo has proposed the aforementioned legislation, which would prohibit homosexual activities sans stoning.

Akinola recognizes that there are concerns about the possible violation of the human rights of individuals affected by the proposal that need to be addressed in "both in the framing of the law and its implementation." He informed the CANA churches that "while the honorable speaker of the House, a Muslim, wanted the immediate and outright passage of the bill, the deputy speaker, an Anglican, persuaded his colleagues to allow full public debate on it."

"[Akinola] is not seeking to victimize or diminish anyone. He is primarily an evangelist and a pastor whose desire is to see all people come to a saving knowledge of Jesus Christ."

It's difficult enough to keep your head as a Christian in Nigeria. For the archbishop to decry legislation that limits "gay rights" would be to expose the entire Christian community in Nigeria to the wrath and violence of the Islamists. Moreover, Akinola has made it quite clear that he believes it is in the best interest of his country, and indeed, of those persons who are living in a homosexual lifestyle, to not "follow the path of license and immorality that we have witnessed in other parts of the world."

The *Times* may not be considered all the news that's fit to print in the Archbishop's Palace in Lagos, but Akinola is well aware of his critics' charges. In a letter to the new CANA churches in the U.S., Akinola wrote, "Sadly, I have heard that some are suggesting that you are now affiliated with a church that seeks to punish homosexual persons. That is a distortion of our true position."

"Every person, regardless of their religion or sexual orientation, is made in the image of God, loved by God, and deserving of the utmost respect," Akinola says. CANA Bishop Martyn Minns adds, "[Akinola] is not seeking to victimize or diminish anyone. He is primarily an evangelist and a pastor whose desire is to see all people come to a saving knowledge of Jesus Christ."

Archbishop Akinola sees individual human beings who need Christ's healing in their lives to become the people they were created to be. The *New York Times* sees an opportunity to promote the gay rights agenda. Who is it who is really diminishing people?

Periodical and Internet Sources Bibliography

The following articles have been selected to supplement the diverse views presented in this chapter.

Bradley Shavit Artson — "Homosexuality and Judaism: Synthesis or Impasse?" American Jewish University, 2010. http://judaism.ajula.edu.

Jonathan Brown — "Homosexuality and Same-Sex Marriage in Islam," Patheos.com, May 12, 2009. www.patheos.com.

Benjamin Cohen — "Comment: Reflections on Yom Kippur and Homosexuality Within Judaism," PinkNews.co.uk, September 29, 2009. www.pinknews.co.uk.

Abdul Khalik — "Islam 'Recognizes Homosexuality,'" *Jakarta Post* (Indonesia), March 28, 2008.

Michael Kirby — "Religious Condemnation of Homosexuals Denies Human Rights," *Age*, June 30, 2008. www.theage.com.au.

LifeSiteNews.com — "Catholic Church Needs to Change on Homosexuality: Leading U.K. Catholic Magazine," February 11, 2010. www.lifesitenews.com.

B.A. Robinson — "The Roman Catholic Church and Homosexuality," ReligiousTolerance.org, January 29, 2010. www.religioustolerance.org.

Bellanvila Sudaththa Thero and Cecil J. Dunne — "Homosexuality, Buddhism and Sri Lankan Society," Groundviews, August 28, 2007. www.groundviews.org.

John-Henry Westen — "Russian Orthodox Patriarch Explains Stand on Homosexuality to Council of Europe," Catholic Exchange, October 4, 2007. http://catholicexchange.com.

GLOBALVIEWPOINTS

CHAPTER 2

Attitudes Toward Homosexuality

Homophobia Is Worsening in Malaysia

Walter L. Williams

Walter L. Williams is a professor of anthropology, history, and gender studies at the University of Southern California, and the founding editor of International Gay & Lesbian Review. *In the following viewpoint, he argues that homophobia in Malaysia has worsened, in large part because of growing cultural conservatism in the Islamic world. As a result, homosexuals in Malaysia face threats to their liberties and even their lives. Williams concludes that homosexuals should be offered asylum in the United States and that the international community should boycott Malaysia for its violations of human rights.*

As you read, consider the following questions:

1. What infamous punishment does Williams say the Taliban in Afghanistan inflicted on homosexuals?

2. According to Zaltun Mohamad Kasim, what laws are gay people often falsely charged with violating in Malaysia?

3. Why does Williams say that it is unlikely that anti-homosexual policies will be changed due to pressure from the media?

Walter L. Williams, "Strategies for Challenging Homophobia in Islamic Malaysia and Secular China," *Nebula*, vol. 6, no. 1, March 2009, pp. 6–10, 12–18. Reproduced by permission.

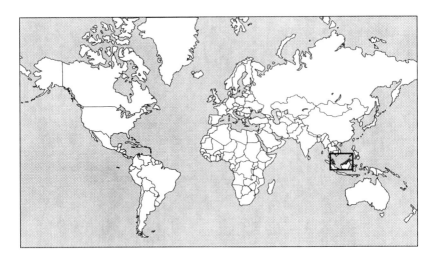

The terrible situation facing LGBT [lesbian, gay, bisexual, and transgender] people in Malaysia is a direct result of the continuation of a British colonial-era sodomy [anal sex] law, but that law's continued enforcement in an independent Malaysia is due to powerful political factors combined with the influence of Islamic religious beliefs. Though in the past many Islamic traditions were not as homophobic as the European Christian tradition, it is ironic that at this point in history many of the most homophobic nations on earth are Islamic. It is also important not to sweep under the rug the fact that dominant Muslim thought today is quite oppressive to gay and lesbian people.

Unequal Prosecution

Malaysia's sodomy law prohibits anal intercourse. This law could theoretically apply to male-female couples, but Malaysia's sodomy law is not applied equally. It has been selectively and systematically enforced to vilify and persecute homosexuals. In Malaysia's Penal Code, Section 377, the sentence for conviction of sodomy is flogging, plus up to twenty years in prison. Victims are flogged with a bamboo cane that is split into several strips. When bamboo is split it has extremely sharp edges, which slice the skin like knives. Flogging is quite bloody, and leaves permanent scars. In addition to Section 337, just to prevent any homosexual from escaping conviction, Section 337A provides for a male to receive up to two years in prison for any act of "gross indecency with another male person." This vague wording allows prosecution for any kind of erotic interaction between two males. This law is explicitly applied only to homosexual behavior among males, and female-female sexual behavior is not specifically mentioned in the penal code, but lesbians also suffer discrimination. There have not been prominent cases of persecution of lesbians in Malaysia, but they are oppressed by other rules which attempt to enforce dress codes and restrictions on women in general. A female who does not conform to gender expectations in Malaysia can expect harassment both from police and from the general population.

The United States State Department 2006 country report on Malaysia concluded that these antigay laws "exist and were enforced. Religious and cultural taboos against homosexuality were widespread." Although the existence of this law in and of itself should be enough to warrant a decision in favor of asylum [in the United States] for a homosexual from Malaysia, there is further evidence that demonstrates the particularly strong and heinous vilification, discrimination and persecution that is happening to homosexuals in Malaysia today.

Though I have not been in Malaysia recently (due to fears about my own safety if I went there), I have continued to do research on the plight of homosexuals in Malaysia. I follow the literature, including periodicals and websites that address and report on gay culture and community issues in Malaysia as well as the rest of Southeast Asia. I have interviewed many gay people from Malaysia, and others who have knowledge of the national climate today. I have a good understanding of the current situation there.

Islam's War on Homosexuals

It is clear from the evidence that in the last decade [1999–2009] the situation has worsened for gay men and lesbians in Malaysia. Partly this is a reflection of a recent crackdown on homosexuals in many Muslim nations. In U.S.-allied Saudi Arabia the punishment that has been meted out for "sodomites" is beheading. In what is probably the understatement of the year, even the U.S. Department of State 2007 country report for Saudi Arabia acknowledged that "sexual activity between two persons of the same gender is punishable by death or flogging. It is illegal for men 'to behave like women' or wear women's clothes and for women to wear men's clothes. There were reports of societal discrimination based on sexual orientation. There were reports of discrimination, physical violence, and harassment toward homosexuals. In October a court in Al-Baha Province sentenced two men to 7,000 lashes each for engaging in sexual intercourse with other men."

Most people know that the Taliban [a militant Islamic group that controlled Afghanistan in the 1990s] in Afghanistan were infamous for forcing accused homosexuals to stand next to a tall brick wall, while a tank pushed the wall over onto them to crush them to death. But even more extreme is the Islamic Republic of Iran. The exiled gay Iranian group Homan estimates that over 4,000 Iranians have been executed for sodomy during the 1980s and 1990s. These executions are often public beheadings or hangings, being stoned to death, being split in half by a sword, being burned alive at the stake, or being thrown from a tall building or mountain cliff. Homan made a statement saying, "Lesbians and gay men living in countries dominated by the New Dark Ages of Islamic fundamentalism cannot afford the liberal luxury of tolerating religious fanaticism. For them, the politically correct arguments about cultural sensitivity smack of surrender to the extremists who jeopardize their freedom and even their lives."

These mass killings of homosexuals, which have been justified in the name of Islam, constitute a major human rights violation of the 20th and early 21st centuries. Even the secular government of Egypt provoked international criticism in 2001 and 2002 due to a campaign of arrests of people who were accused of homosexuality. Many of those convicted of participating in consensual sexual acts with another person of the same sex were sentenced to prison for several years. In 2005 in northern Nigeria a man accused of homosexuality was sentenced to die under that territory's Islamic shariah law. The list of examples could go on. In short, for any country where fundamentalist Islamic influences are dominant, homosexuals are in grave danger of being killed or imprisoned.

It is clear from the evidence that in the last decade the situation has worsened for gay men and lesbians in Malaysia.

Homophobia as a Political Tool

Malaysia's government defines itself as a government based on "Islamic principles," as a way of avoiding the limits placed on constitutional democracy. Its recently retired prime minister, Mahathir [bin] Mohamad, held massive political power for 22 years. In 1998 Islamic homophobia and Malaysian politics intertwined as Malaysia's Deputy Prime Minister Anwar Ibrahim made a major break with Mahathir due to his economic policies, and pressured him to institute democratic reforms. The prime minister responded by charging that Anwar had sex with two men. Anwar refused to be intimidated by what he called an untrue smear, and led protests against the dictatorial policies of the government. Mahathir then used the existence of the sodomy law to have his major political rival arrested.

While in custody, Anwar was severely beaten by the chief of police. Two men testified at his trial that Anwar had sex with them. But both of them later recanted their stories, and admitted that they had been pressured by government officials and police to make the accusation of sodomy. Mahathir obviously believed that the charge of homosexuality would be so damning that most people in Malaysia would withdraw their support for Anwar and his call for democratic reforms would be discredited. While many Malaysians supported the deputy prime minister, and joined protests on his behalf, most of them have done so only because they believe he did not really commit homosexual acts.

In reaction to the Anwar case in 2000 a report by the International Bar Association, after its on-site study of justice in Malaysia, concluded that "the extremely powerful executive in Malaysia has not acted with due regard for the essential elements of a free and democratic society based on the rule of law."

Prime Minister Mahathir has made repeated attacks on homosexuals. These attacks are not marginal to his argument, but are a central point of his rhetoric.

In response to mounting international criticism, the government established a National Human Rights Commission, but the man placed in charge of this commission is a supporter of Prime Minister Mahathir. The commission defines human rights solely as those provided for in the Malaysian constitution, and this does not include rights for homosexuals. There is no challenge to Malaysia's sodomy law, which criminalizes all those who engage in same-sex relationships.

Instead of retreating, Mahathir's government justified its position on Anwar by stiffening their attacks on homosexuality. Government officials joined in a rising chorus of condemnations of homosexuality. In *Time* magazine's Web edition of September 26, 2000, Abdul Kadir Che Kob, a top government official at Malaysia's Islamic Affairs Department, was interviewed. In this interview, Abdul Kadir said: "Homosexuality is forbidden in Islam. It is a crime worse than murder. Homosexuals are shameless people." When asked by the interviewer if people should not have the right to choose who they want to be with, Abdul Kadir replied: "What right are you talking about? This is a sin, end of story. How can men have sex with men? God did not make them this way. This is all Western influence." He explained that police use anonymous tips to trap homosexuals: "Usually people give us precise information like where these men are. We then go to the place, say, a hotel room. We knock and force them to open the door, but they are usually fully clothed by then. We still charge them for attempting to commit homosexual acts. We charge them in court, but before that we put them through what we call Islamic counseling sessions. They recite the Koran every day and we will tell them they have committed a grave sin. We have to tell these people they are doing something very wrong in the eyes of Allah. It is a major sin."

Prime Minister Mahathir has made repeated attacks on homosexuals. These attacks are not marginal to his argument, but are a central point of his rhetoric. For example, in his speech to the General Assembly of the United Malays National Organisation (UMNO), on June 19, 2003, the prime minister ominously titled a section of his address "The Dangers We Face." He stated that the main danger facing Malaysia's future is a campaign by Europeans and Americans to force Malaysians to adopt Western freedoms. He said, "Our minds, our culture, our religion, and other things will become the target. In the cultural and social fields they want to see unlimited freedom for the individual. . . . They accept the practice of free sex, including sodomy, as a right. . . . The culture and values which they will force us to accept will be hedonism, unlimited quest for pleasure, the satisfaction of base desires, particularly sexual desires."

Malaysia Fights Against International Rights for Homosexuals

With this kind of rhetoric from the prime minister, Malaysian officials at the United Nations [UN] took a leadership role in denouncing sexual minorities. For example, during a United Nations General Assembly session on the HIV/AIDS epidemic, delegates from Malaysia were highly critical of any recognition of sexual minorities. That is, they were even prepared to prevent effective efforts to address the epidemic, if it meant recognizing gay AIDS organizations that were attempting to curtail the spread of HIV. The international watchdog group, Human Rights Watch, highlighted Malaysia in its *World Report 2002: Special Issues and Campaigns*. This report pointed out that government "inspectors have forced AIDS prevention groups in Malaysia to stop distributing condoms, at a time when HIV infections are rising."

A year later, Malaysia's government took the lead in killing a resolution in the United Nations that called for the end of executions and imprisonment for homosexual behavior. According to England's August 25, 2003, issue of the *Guardian*, "A landmark UN vote on homosexual human rights was on Thursday derailed at the last minute by an alliance of disapproving Muslim countries—Malaysia, Pakistan, Egypt, Libya and Saudi Arabia. . . . Same-sex relations are harshly repressed in Bangladesh, Egypt, Malaysia, and Pakistan." . . .

In addition to all this that is happening on the national level, Malaysian women's rights activist Zaltun Mohamad Kasim points out that local laws are becoming even more repressive. She has been speaking out publicly about the dangers of increasingly strident attacks on sexuality by Muslim leaders. She gave a speech at an international human rights conference in 2004 in which she stated that in Malaysia, "Sexuality [is] under attack. . . . Inspired by the ideology of Islamic conservatism, there is a growing obsession with . . . guarding and policing morality." One of the most insidious new laws, that was passed with hardly any objection, provides that "anyone who gives, propagates, and/or disseminates any opinion contrary to any fatwa [Islamic directive] in force commits a criminal offense." Since a fatwa issued by Muslim leaders states that homosexuality is a sin, anyone in Malaysia who tries to suggest otherwise is subject to arrest merely for stating their opinion. . . .

Gay people, [Kasim] points out, are often falsely charged with violations of prostitution laws, and other laws that are deemed to protect public morality, simply because homosexuality "is demonized as un-Islamic, unnatural, disgusting, and a crime worse than murder. . . . They become vulnerable to legal prosecution under both the civil and shariah legal systems as well as being easy targets for public persecution, sexual and physical violence, and harassment. . . . The growing conservatism in the country has also given rise to self-appointed vigilante Islamist groups or individuals in the universities, the workplace, and also in public spaces, who have taken it upon themselves to harass and police other individuals and groups." Some non-masculine males who are suspected of being homosexual have been expelled from Malaysian universities "and told to come back when they become 'real men.'"

Since a fatwa issued by Muslim leaders states that homosexuality is a sin, anyone in Malaysia who tries to suggest otherwise is subject to arrest merely for stating their opinion.

Isolated and Alone

Gay people have no one to speak up for them in Malaysia. Even academic researchers are intimidated by being dependent upon government appointments and funding. Faculty at Malaysian universities are prohibited from engaging in political debates. For example, several teachers were dismissed by the government's Teaching Service Commission just for assigning

The Media and Homosexuality in Malaysia

The media representation on the issue of homosexuality in Malaysia is negatively skewed as 74% of the articles are framed/portrayed in a negative way. . . . The media reporting on homosexuality perpetuates a negative attitude of public opinion towards the phenomenon. By emphasizing or frequently mentioning the issue in a negative manner, the media increase the salience of this issue among the public. . . .

Negative words such as "immoral act", "illegal", "not halal" [in accord with Islamic law], "criminal offence" and "harsh punishment" in the articles leave an impression to the readers that homosexuality activities are not acceptable and if they're caught, they will be punished. The media, by portraying homosexuality as an act that is punishable or which leads to social illness, generally informs the public what line of thought to follow.

Ponmalar N. Alagappar and Karamjeet Kaur,
"The Representation of Homosexuality—
A Content Analysis in a Malaysian Newspaper,"
Language in India, vol. 9, October 10, 2009.
www.languageinindia.com.

students to debate political policies in a debate competition. Without any public discourse on the subject of equal rights for homosexuals, there is little opportunity for changing the attitudes of the public or government authorities.

In this context of rising intolerance, Malaysia's Information Minister Datuk Mohamed Rahmat announced a policy that the government will not allow any known gay man, lesbian, or transvestite to appear on television programs. He stated: "Any artist who is proven to be a gay will come under the ban. We do not want to encourage any form of homosexuality in our society." This policy is frighteningly similar to laws passed by the Nazis in 1930s Germany, prohibiting Jews from appearing in any of the mass media. These laws proved to be a prelude to the concentration camp policies that followed.

Without any public discourse on the subject of equal rights for homosexuals, there is little opportunity for changing the attitudes of the public or government authorities.

The chances of these policies being changed due to pressure from the media [are] very slim, because publishers must apply annually to the government for a permit to publish their newspapers, books, or magazines. The fact that most of the major media in Malaysia are owned by top government officials means that the media do not challenge any government policy. In addition, the government censorship board prevents publication of "malicious news," and censors discussion of any kind of sexual matters in the press. The *Sun*, a leading newspaper in Malaysia, even went so far as to say on August 13, 2007, that "the government should strip the citizenship of Malaysians who betray the country by making comments that humiliate Islam."

Therefore, since the Malaysian government considers homosexuality to be an affront to Islam, any news relating to gay and lesbian rights, especially including calls for ending discrimination against homosexuals, is suppressed. For example, on February 22, 2006, the main newspaper the *Malay Mail* in a front-page story not only did not criticize the government for police raids on gay businesses, but even joined in on the raids by taking and printing photographs of the men who were arrested. In lurid tabloid style, the article compared gays to prostitutes. . . .

The fact that homosexuals are so commonly arrested is itself a sentence of punishment. A person who is arrested for a crime in Malaysia often has to wait in jail for a long time, sometimes up to eight years, before being brought to trial. Guards regularly beat prisoners. Torture of prisoners is justified by the sentence of being flogged with a cane that is often meted out by the courts. This practice of caning is so severe that prisoners often faint from the pain, and are left with permanent scars. In the case of prisoners who are homosexual, the extensive publicity regarding government condemnation of homosexuality has sent the message to the police and others that persecution of homosexuals is acceptable. . . .

The statement often made, that homosexuality "is worse than murder," and "an affront to Islam," is a real and present danger for any person who is even suspected of homosexual proclivities.

Asylum for Malaysian Homosexuals

United States immigration policy allows political asylum to be granted to an applicant based on their realistic fear of "persecution on account of membership in a particular social group." Male and female homosexuals definitely constitute such a social group in the context of government and religious persecution in Malaysia. Even if an individual is not convicted of a specific sexual act, they can still be persecuted based upon their perceived membership in the social group of homosexuals. They do not even have the freedom of association to gather with other gay-identified persons in a social setting, without persecution. Even sitting in a car, a public park, or anywhere that police suspect two or more people of being homosexuals, leaves one open to police harassment, arrest, and/or torture. Even if they were not engaged in sexual activity, merely being perceived as gay by itself is enough for the police to take such actions. Both males and females are persecuted on the basis of their *perceived* membership in this social group.

Even if government-sponsored persecution might abate in the future, there is still the probability that Muslim Fundamentalists will continue to try to "wipe out" homosexuals. The statement often made, that homosexuality "is worse than murder," and "an affront to Islam," is a real and present danger for any person who is even suspected of homosexual proclivities.

All my recent research shows that conditions for homosexuals in Malaysia are quite precarious. Things are getting worse rather than better, and there is no evidence of any turnaround potential for the foreseeable future. As Malaysian human rights activist Farish Noor sounded the alarm in 2005: "It should be painfully obvious to all by now that there are very real repressive undercurrents in Malaysian society."

The negative attitudes, discrimination and persecution being experienced by Malaysian gay people today is a direct result of the combination of religious attitudes and governmental politics. Defining homosexuality as criminal "sodomy," imprisonment, censorship of media discussions of the issue, and police oppression together constitute a pattern of government-sponsored persecution that is impossible to deny.

Immigration and asylum for LGBT people today, just as it was for Jews fleeing Nazi persecution in the 1930s and 1940s, is an important moral question for our time.

With this being the case, I call upon the initiation of a massive boycott of those nations that are actively persecuting sexual minorities. The Malaysian government is conducting a major campaign to encourage tourism in Malaysia. Gay and lesbian travel agents have to be the first to say that they will not encourage tourism to Malaysia until the government changes its homophobic policies. Don't buy Malaysian products, and protest American corporations that do business with Malaysia. This applies to every other homophobic government in the world as well.

It is important to publicize this persecution, and not allow it to be swept under the rug because of religion. Sooner or later, homophobic governments will be forced to accommodate to the emerging global consensus that such persecution, even if religiously based, is wrong. I remain an optimist, and having seen such dramatic change in China [where homophobia has much diminished], as well as in other countries, I feel that change is possible in the Islamic world as well. There are some Muslim nations that are not actively persecuting homosexuals, and they can be the model for change by the homophobic governments. But though I am ultimately optimistic I also know it will be a long struggle. In the meantime, we owe it to the people who are being discriminated against to do everything we can to help them escape from the oppressive conditions under which they have to live. Immigration and asylum for LGBT people today, just as it was for Jews fleeing Nazi persecution in the 1930s and 1940s, is an important moral question for our time. I am proud to have made my contribution in this area, and call upon all other rational people who oppose discrimination to do likewise.

In India, Homosexuality Is Treated with Benign Neglect

Sudhir Kakar

Sudhir Kakar is a psychoanalyst and writer who lives in Goa, India. In the following viewpoint, he argues that in India few men see themselves as homosexuals, though same-sex intercourse is not uncommon. Kakar notes that homosexual acts were traditionally seen as unimportant as long as traditional family structures and procreation were not threatened. Thus, he concludes, male homosexuality has generally been tolerated as long as it remains invisible. Lesbianism, he notes, has been treated more harshly.

As you read, consider the following questions:

1. What are the dhurrati panthis and the komat panthis according to gay activist Ashok Row Kavi?
2. According to Kakar, what is a kliba?
3. In princely courts in northern India, why does Kakar say that homosexual relationships were safer than relationships with mistresses?

In India, except for a few people belonging to the English-speaking elite in metropolitan centers, mostly in the higher echelons of advertising, fashion, design, fine and performing arts, men (and women) with same-sex partners neither iden-

Sudhir Kakar, "Homosexuality and the Indian," *Little India*, August 17, 2007. Reproduced by permission.

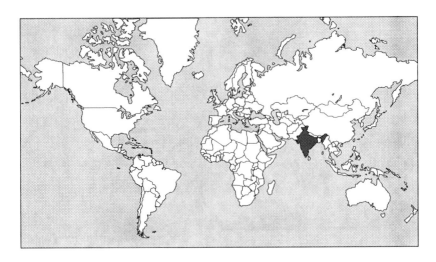

tify themselves as homosexuals nor admit their sexual preference, often even to themselves. Many men—some married—
have had or continue to have sex with other men; but only a
miniscule minority are willing to recognize themselves as homosexual.

Same-Sex Love, but Not Homosexuality

The assertion that there are hardly any homosexuals in India
and yet there is considerable same-sex involvement seems
contradictory, yet simple to reconcile. Sex between men especially among friends or within the family during adolescence
and youth, is not regarded as sex, but masti, an exciting, erotic
playfulness, with overtones of the mast elephant in heat [male
elephants periodically experience mast, a hormone surge causing aggressive behavior].

Outside male friendship, it is a way to satisfy an urgent
bodily need or, for some, to make money. Sex, on the other
hand, is the serious business of procreation within marriage.
Almost all men who have sex with other men will get married, even if many continue to have sex with men after marriage. Sexual relations with men are not a source of conflict as
long as the person believes he is not a homosexual in the

sense of having an exclusive preference for men and does not compromise his masculine identity by not marrying and refusing to produce children.

As a recent study tells us, "Even effeminate men who have a strong desire for receiving penetrative sex are likely to consider their role as husbands and fathers to be more important in their self-identification than their homosexual behavior."

Almost all men who have sex with other men will get married, even if many continue to have sex with men after marriage.

The cultural ideology that strongly links sexual identity with the ability to marry and procreate does indeed lessen the conflict around homosexual behavior. Yet for many it also serves the function of masking their sexual orientation, of denying them the possibility of an essential aspect of self-knowledge. Those with a genuine homosexual orientation subconsciously feel compelled to maintain an emotional distance in their homosexual encounters and thus struggle against the search for love and intimacy which, besides the press of sexual desire, motivated these encounters in the first place.

Homosexual Denial

The "homosexual denial," as some might call it, is facilitated by Indian culture in many ways. A man's behavior has to be really flagrant, such as that of the cross-dressing hijras [males who refer to themselves as and dress as women, or as a "third sex," neither male nor female] to excite interest or warrant comment. Some find elaborate cultural defenses to deny their homosexual orientation. The gay activist Ashok Row Kavi tells us about the dhurrati panthis, men who have sex with other men because the semen inside them makes them twice as manly and capable of really satisfying their wives. Then there are the komat panthis who like to give oral sex, but will not let themselves be touched. Some of these men are revered teachers, "gurus," in body-building gymnasiums, who believe they will become exceptionally powerful by performing oral sex on younger men. Both will be horrified to be called homosexual.

In general, classical Hinduism is significantly silent on the subject of homoeroticism. In contrast to the modern notion of homosexuality, which is defined by a preference for a partner of the same sex, queerness in ancient India was determined by atypical sexual or gender behavior. Some of our contemporary attitudes towards homosexuality go back in time to ancient India, where it was the homosexual (but not homosexual activity) who evoked society's scorn. As in several other societies, such as in Middle East and Latin America, the active partner in a homoerotic encounter was not stigmatized as much as the passive partner [that is, the person penetrated]. It was what you did, whether you were active or passive, and not with whom you did it (man or woman) that defined acceptability. The *Kamasutra*'s [an ancient Hindu text about human sexual behavior] man-about-town who uses the masseur's mouth for sexual pleasure is thus not considered "queer"; the masseur is.

Actually, in classical India, the disparagement for the homosexual was not devoid of compassion. The homosexual belonged to a deficient class of men called kliba in Sanskrit [a classical Indian language]; deficient because he is unable to produce male offspring. The word (which has traditionally been translated as eunuch, but almost certainly did not mean eunuch) was a catchall term to include someone who was sterile, impotent, castrated, a transvestite, a man who had oral sex with other men, who had anal sex as a recipient, a man with mutilated or deficient sexual organs, a man who produced only female children, or, finally, a hermaphrodite. In short, kliba is a term traditional Hindus coined to describe a man who is in their terms sexually dysfunctional (or in ours, sexually challenged). Kliba is not a term that exists any longer, but some of its remnant—the perception of a deficiency, and the combination of pity, dismay and a degree of disdain toward a man who is unable to marry and produce children— continues to cling to the Indian homosexual.

In general, classical Hinduism is significantly silent on the subject of homoeroticism.

It is instructive that the *Kamasutra* the main source of information on ancient sexuality, does not use the term kliba at all. It mentions sodomy [anal sex] in only one passage, and that in the context of heterosexual and not homosexual sex: "The people in the South indulge in 'sex below,' even anally." (In general Southerners have a pretty poor reputation in this book composed in the North, and it could be that their geographical position suggested their sexual position in this passage: down under). In the *Kamasutra*, fellatio [oral sex] is regarded as the defining male homosexual act.

Homosexuality and Rebirth

In *Same-Sex Love in India*, Ruth Vanita argues that the relative tolerance, the gray area between simple acceptance and outright rejection of homosexual attraction, can be primarily attributed to the Hindu concept of rebirth. Instead of condemning the couple, others can explain their mutual attraction as involuntary, because it is caused by attachment in a previous birth. This attachment is presumed to have the character of "unfinished business," which needed to be brought to a resolution in the present birth.

In ancient texts, folktales and in daily conversations, mismatched lovers, generally those with vast differences in status (a fisherman or an untouchable falling in love with a princess), are reluctantly absolved of blame and the union gradually accommodated, because it is viewed as destined from a former

The Hijras of India

In India, hijras are viewed as an institutionalized "third sex" that has always existed. They are particularly associated with the worship of Bahuchara Mata, a version of the Mother Goddess, for whose sake they undergo emasculation. In return, the goddess gives them the power to bless people with fertility. Their presence in society is justified by many Hindu myths. For example, one of the forms of the god Shiva is that of Ardhanarisvara, half man, half woman, who represents Shiva united with his shakti, or female creative power. . . . Hijras clearly have an accepted status within Hindu mythology and culture.

Kabir Altaf, "The Hijras of India," Chay Magazine, *August 1, 2008. http://chaymagazine.org.*

birth. When a brave homosexual couple defies all convention by openly living together, its tolerance by the two families and the social surround generally takes place in the framework of the rebirth theory. In 1987, when two policewomen in the state of Madhya Pradesh in central India got "married," a cause celebre in the Indian media, the explanation often heard from those who could no longer regard them as "just good friends sharing living accommodations" was that one of them must have been a man in a previous birth and the couple prematurely separated by a cruel fate.

In ancient India, homosexual activity itself was ignored or stigmatized as inferior, but never actively persecuted. In the dharmashastras [Hindu law books], male homoerotic activity is punished, albeit mildly: a ritual bath or the payment of a small fine was often sufficient atonement. This did not change materially in spite of the advent of Islam, which unequivocally condemns homosexuality as a serious crime. Muslim theologians in India held that the Prophet advocated the severest punishment for sodomy. Islamic culture in India, though, also had a Persian cast wherein homoeroticism is celebrated in literature. In Sufi [an Islamic tradition of worship] mystical poetry, both in Persian and later in Urdu [an Indian/Pakistani language], the relationship between the divine and humans was expressed in homoerotic metaphors.

Inevitably, the mystical was also enacted at the human level. At least among the upper classes of Muslims, among "men of refinement," pederasty [a relationship between an older man and a younger boy] became an accepted outlet for a man's erotic promptings, as long as he continued to fulfill his duties as a married man. Emperor Babur's autobiography is quite clear on his indifferent love for his wife and his preference for a lad. We also know that until the middle of the twentieth century, when the princely states were incorporated into an independent India, there was a strong tradition of homosexuality in many princely courts in north India. The homosexual relationships were much safer than relationships with mistresses whose children could be the source of endless divisive rivalries.

In ancient India, homosexual activity itself was ignored or stigmatized as inferior, but never actively persecuted.

It seems that the contemporary perception of homosexual activity, primarily in images of sodomy, can be traced back to the Muslim period of Indian history. As we saw, the classical Hindu image of homosexual activity is in terms of fellatio. In the *Kamasutra*, for instance, the fellatio technique of the closeted man of "third nature" (the counterpart of the kliba in other Sanskrit texts) is discussed in considerable sensual detail. I would venture to add that one reason Hindu homosexuals regard sodomy with considerable ambivalence, exciting and

repulsive at the same time, has also to do with their strong taboos around issues of purity versus pollution; the mouth is
cleaner than the anus.

Lesbians in India

If male homosexuals make themselves invisible, then lesbians
simply do not exist in Indian society—or so it seems. Again, it
is not that Indians are unaware of lesbian activity. Yet this activity is never seen as a matter of personal choice, a possibility
that is theoretically, if reluctantly, granted to "deficient" men,
the men of "third nature" in ancient India. Lesbian activity, on
the other hand, is invariably seen as an outcome of the lack of
sexual satisfaction in unmarried women, widows or women
stuck in unhappy, sexless marriages. This is true even in creative depiction of lesbian activity in fiction or movies. In
Deepa Mehta's 1996 movie *Fire*, which sparked a major controversy, with Hindu activists setting fire to cinema halls because the movie showed two women having an affair, both
women turn to each other only because they are deeply unhappy in their marriages.

In ancient India, lesbian activity is described in the *Kamasutra* at the beginning of the chapter on harems where many
women live together in the absence of men. What the queens
have is just one king, preoccupied with affairs of state, to go
around. Since none of the kings can be the god Krishna, who
is reputed to have satisfied each one of his sixteen thousand
wives every night, the women use dildos, as well as bulbs,
roots or fruits that have the form of the male organ. The im-
plication is that lesbian activity takes place only in the absence
of the "real thing." There are hints on other kinds of lesbian
activity in the ancient law books: a woman who corrupts a
virgin is to be punished by having two of her fingers cut
off—a pointer to what the male author thinks two women do
in bed. The harsh punishment is not for the activity itself but
for the "deflowering," the heinous crime of robbing a young

girl of her chastity. Not surprisingly, it seems that female homosexuality was punished more severely than homosexuality among men; out of concern for the protection of women's virginity and sexual purity, traditionalists would say; to exercise control over women's sexual choice and activity, modern feminists would counter.

If male homosexuals make themselves invisible, then lesbians simply do not exist in Indian society—or so it seems.

In general, then, India has a tradition of "benign neglect" of alternate sexualities, a tradition that is very much a part of the Indian mind. The laws against homosexual activity, such as the act of 1861 [which made gay sex a crime; repealed in 2009], are all examples of a repressive Victorian moral code. It is ironic that reactionaries, both Hindu and Muslim, who reject homosexuality as a decadent Western phenomenon subscribe to the same foreign code that is so alien to the Indian tradition. The Indian tradition of indifference or deliberate ignorance is also incompatible with the model of the Western gay movement, which is beginning to make inroads into our metropolises. In its insistence on the politics of a gay identity, of a proud or at least defiant assertion of homosexual identity, this movement is beginning to compel the rest of society to confront the issue publicly.

Depictions of Gay Men in Japanese Comics for Women Are Not Homophobic

Wim Lunsing

Wim Lunsing is an anthropologist who has been affiliated with the University of Tokyo and the University of Copenhagen. In the following viewpoint, he notes that BLB (boys love boys) and yaoi manga—Japanese comics by women for women that depict gay male relationships—are often criticized as homophobic. However, Lunsing argues that many gay men actually enjoy BLB and yaoi manga and that depictions of homosexual men in gay manga are not that different from those in BLB and yaoi. He concludes that yaoi and BLB do not promote harmful attitudes toward gay men.

As you read, consider the following questions:

1. Why does Mark J. McLelland say that *shōjo manga* depictions are not representative of actual gay existence?

2. What does *yaoi* stand for?

3. Why does Mizoguchi Akiko think that BLB *manga* depictions are homophobic, according to Lunsing?

A number of papers in English have discussed the genre of *shōjo manga* [Japanese girls' comics] known as BLB (boy loves boy) *manga* in which gay male characters figure promi-

Wim Lunsing, "Yaoi Ronsō: Discussing Depictions of Male Homosexuality in Japanese Girls' Comics, Gay Comics and Gay Pornography," *Intersections: Gender, History and Culture in the Asian Context*, vol. 12, January 2006. Reproduced by permission.

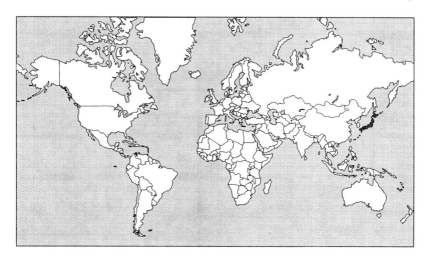

nently and which were first published in the 1970s. However, little attention has been paid to developments in the 1980s, let alone the 1990s, resulting in an outdated depiction of the genre, with, for instance, a stress on the foreignness or other-worldliness of the situations described. [Researcher Mark J.] McLelland takes the discussion further to include newer *manga* situated in the present but insists that the depictions are equally not representative of actual gay existence, as they are over-romantic. The same point is made about Japanese films and television shows depicting homosexuality, which, like the *manga*, are mostly aimed at a female audience. Answers to questions such as who reads the genre and why have been sought in women's resistance to patriarchy, ignoring the fact that there are also many gay male readers. . . .

Yaoi stands for **ya**ma nashi, **o**chi nashi, **i**mi nashi, which means 'no climax [as in the climax of a story], no plot, no meaning.' The genre supposedly consists only of sex scenes, which often are characterised to some extent by violence, hence also the joking interpretation of the meaning of *yaoi* as *yamete, oshiri ga itai* [stop, my ass hurts]. The feminist *manga* specialist Tanigawa Tamae estimated, based on figures of fan circles' membership and comic fair participants, that about

100,000 people are fans of the genre, most of them young women. *Yaoi* critic, Satō Masaki, mentions a figure of 200,000 and the lesbian Mizoguchi Akiko even gives the figure of 500,000 people as forming the core of the readership, based on an investigation by the *yaoi* specialist Kurihara Chiyo of the number of magazines published. The discrepancy in the figures may partly be explained by the fact that the term *yaoi* is used with varying meanings. Generally, the magazine *June*, which probably refers to Jean Genet (*June* in Japanese sounding similar to the Japanese way of rendering Genet), is presented as exemplary of *yaoi*. However, if one looks at the contents, one will find that they can hardly be described as concentrating on sex only and lacking plots. In fact, *manga* appearing in *June* have much in common with the earlier works of Yamagishi, . . . and the like as well as the later social realism of . . . Akisato. In practice, the term *yaoi* is most commonly used inclusively to refer to all BLB *manga*, which has evidently led to the high figures of *yaoi* fans. . . .

Yaoi May Harm Gay Men

In 1992, Satō Masaki, a gay activist/civil servant/drag queen, harshly attacked *yaoi*—using the term in a personifying manner: He attacked women who draw and read *yaoi*—with the phrase: '*yaoi nan tte shinde shimaeba ii*' [that *yaoi* may die]. He did this in the *minikomishi* [small-scale, noncommercial magazine] *Choisir*, a feminist magazine devoted to the discussion of female sexuality by women. He felt that his human rights as a gay man were harmed by women drawing and enjoying *yaoi manga*. He compared them to the 'dirty old men' [*hentai jijii*] who watch pornography including women engaging in sexual activities with each other. In addition, he accused *yaoi* of creating and having a skewed image of gay men as beautiful and handsome and regarding gay men who do not fit that image and tend to 'hide in the dark' as 'garbage' [*gomi*]. In addition, he attacked them for creating the 'gay boom', a media wave of interest in gay issues sparked by the women's magazine *Crea*, which, according to him, did nothing for gay men at large.

Women who enjoy *yaoi* responded to this attack. Takamatsu Hisako, calling herself *yaoi* according to Satō's definition, though she dislikes the term, first pointed out that Satō's usage of the term was not correct, as he included all BLB *manga*, rather than the subgenre of *yaoi* with its focus on explicit sex. Nevertheless, she accepted Satō's broader usage for the sake of the argument. She pointed out that for her boys' love *manga* were liberating in the sense that, unlike in heterosexual stories, in the case of *yaoi*, for a character to look at another's body meant also to have his own body looked at. Whereas in straight material the woman was always the object and the man the viewer—in *yaoi* this role division did not exist. She agreed, however, that, as a reader of *yaoi*, she was similar to dirty old men looking at pornography featuring women.

Yanagita Akiko made a slightly different argument. She recounted the fact that when she was in high school she felt that she was an 'absurdly sick being' [*tonde mo nai kimochiwarui sonzai*]. She felt that her interest in *yaoi* did not relate to gay men in particular but to people in general. She claimed that she did not particularly like the depictions of beautiful gay men but rather liked particular characters in the *manga* as well as particular real-life women. To her, the interesting point of *yaoi manga* was that they inevitably concerned men/boys who had individuality [*kosei*]. The fact that the boys/men in *yaoi* are depicted as beautiful she related to the fact that women in *shōjo manga* are also depicted as beautiful, a mere characteristic of the entire genre of *shōjo manga*. She felt shocked that Satō even read *yaoi* as something related to himself as a gay man. The reason why she wrote and read *yaoi* had nothing to do with an interest in gay men but with the fact that she could not cope with heterosexual depictions, in

Why Do Women Like Yaoi?

The most common answer is that yaoi is simply the mirror image of lesbian porn for men: It's normal for straight folks, male and female, to fantasize about the opposite sex in homoerotic situations. Fantasies that don't include one-self (or anyone of one's own sex) as part of the scenario often provide a safe, comforting way to explore heterosexual desires.

Shaenon K. Garrity,
"Yaoi for Parents, A Crash Course in Boys' Love,"
Graphic Novel Review, September 21, 2009.
www.graphicnovelreview.com.

which the woman always ended up being the underdog, nor with depictions of woman-woman relations because of her own confusion in relation to her feelings for women, in which case she could not help, when imagining sex, but to think of raping them. She admitted that what she wanted to draw and read in *yaoi*, was probably not agreeable to gay men, but then, she wondered, what *does* Satō want 'us' to draw?

In straight material the woman was always the object and the man the viewer—in yaoi *this role division did not exist.*

What *Yaoi* Means for Women

Satō dismissed this question as too stupid for consideration. He never asked women to draw *manga* featuring male homosexuality in the first place and suggested that *yaoi* think for themselves. Later, however, he gave an indication of how he would like to see gay men depicted. He wrote that he was very impressed by the skill Takaguchi Satosumi showed in her story *Kouun Danshi [Rakkii Kun]*. . . . He read it with great pleasure until in the end, when, to his distress, one of the characters died—an extremely common way to end any sort of Japanese story—and the remaining character decided that he should marry and start a family, which Satō read as a denial of the validity of gay lifestyles. The message that the story in the end conveyed to Satō was that gay men cannot be happy. Later he admitted to liking BLB *manga* but he remained insistent that *yaoi* are homophobic and debase the tradition of BLB *manga*. Good *manga* must not 'incite an escape from reality' but 'make reality easier to live in.' He also made no distinction between *yaoi* and the women who like to court gay men as friends, called *okoge* . . . , who also objectify handsome gay men. However, as long as *yaoi* remained small scale and something for personal pleasure, he did not find any harm in it. The problems arose once the genre entered into the mainstream—as, undeniably, it has. In March 2002, Tokyo's largest book store Kinokuniya had a BLB *manga* fair on its ground floor.

Tanigawa Tamae, criticising the women who agreed with Satō that they were like dirty old men, counterattacked Satō for using his position as a gay man to attack a group such as *yaoi* who are much weaker, since, unlike gay men, they are not recognised in their own right. She maintained that for gay men it was perfectly possible to put the images they want out in the media and that *yaoi manga* do nothing to prevent them from doing that. She regarded *yaoi* authors and readers as victims of patriarchy, which prevented them from loving themselves as women. I believe that the admittance of being guilty of hurting gay men by Takamatsu and Yanagita is too easy and that they fell into the trap of siding with the supposedly weaker group of gay men instead of properly analysing their motives. Their inability to enjoy existing depictions of heterosexual activity combined with unease about female-female sexuality suggests, indeed, that female *yaoi* fans had the larger problem when it came to dealing with their own sexuality. . . .

I found that many of my gay informants were not only familiar with BLB manga, *but read them voraciously.*

Homophobia in BLB *Manga* Is Overstated

In Japan, discussions of BLB *manga* tend to focus on particular features of some *manga*. Satō's opinion that they are homophobic is shared by [*manga* critic] Mizoguchi Akiko, though not for exactly the same reasons. She found that the characters in BLB *manga*, while falling in love with a man, often maintain that they are straight [*nonke*]. She interprets this as homophobia, as the characters are phobic towards a gay identity; they maintain that they are essentially straight but just developed erotic and loving feelings for one particular man. Thus, they distance themselves from gay men, who, supposedly, have feelings of love towards any man, or at least multiple men. . . .

In today's Japan, the homophobia that Mizoguchi describes is commonplace and, moreover, when men regard themselves as gay it is not uncommon for them not to encompass homosexuality as their mainstay of identity, which in itself need not to be a problem. Misogyny is common, as are depictions of violence in combination with sex. I found that many of my gay informants [that is, people the author spoke with in Japan in his capacity as an anthropologist] were not only familiar with BLB *manga* but read them voraciously from the moment they came on the market in the mid-1970s. Even if the stories were set in alien contexts, the gay informants could relate their situation and feelings to the *manga*. While Satō felt that the stories were impeding a positive validation of gay lifestyles, other gay men evaluated them in a more positive manner. The fact that some stories may include homophobia did not prevent them from reading them with pleasure. Even the romantic *Kaze to Ki no Uta,* in which the main protagonist Gilbert is nothing but a sex toy who gets raped over and over again and in which homosexuality is definitely not placed in a positive light, was often pointed out as a must-read by gay friends. I felt they were right, as for me, too, it was utterly compelling, to a similar extent as the work of Tagame Gengorō, in which men are forced to be sex toys for the satisfaction of others, regardless of what sexual identity they may have.

Satō's accusation that female BLB fans are homophobic is of a complex nature. Based on personal contacts, interviews and participant observation, I believe that there are several ways in which women read BLB *manga.* As Satō agrees, initially BLB *manga* were an important innovation in the otherwise asexual genre of *shōjo manga.* Love between boys was a means for women to reconsider, or even to begin considering, their own sexuality. It mattered less that the stories concerned boys than that they concerned sex. . . .

A Positive Influence on Male Sexuality

The *iyarashii* [disgusting] sex in BLB *manga* can be liberating for gay men's sexuality in a manner similar to gay *manga.* This can be regarded as a positively queer influence on male sexuality. Discussions taking place on BLB *manga* are irrelevant to the majority of the readers, who simply enjoy what they read. Moreover, the recent popularity of BLB *manga* in China and Korea shows that their impact is not limited to audiences who grew up in a Japanese cultural context. It is to be hoped that BLB *manga* will remain beyond the scrutiny of the new Japanese law against child pornography and that Korean government efforts to ban the genre will be thwarted, since they are a form of art and art should be free. Critiques such as those of Satō and Mizoguchi entail the risk of leading to the establishment of norms on how male homosexuality must be depicted, which would result in a normalised, stale representation of male homosexuality. Obviously, this would be utterly un-queer and contrary to the performative acts in which identity and activity are not related in a linear manner—a characteristic of Japanese sexualities. Many Japanese gay men appear to use depictions of gay men that are not (meant to be) positive and supportive, by seeing them as performances that can in turn enhance their own lives.

Western Evangelicals Have Encouraged Homophobia in Uganda

John Moore

John Moore is the host of Moore in the Morning *on NewsTalk 1010 in Toronto. In the following viewpoint, he reports that three American Evangelical Christians have spoken in Uganda against homosexuality. Moore argues that the Evangelicals' mix of pseudoscience and bigotry has helped to promote dangerous antigay legislation in Uganda. Moore believes that the failure of Christians to strongly condemn this legislation, as well as their failure to strongly condemn the persecution of gays elsewhere in the world, is sinful.*

As you read, consider the following questions:

1. Who were the three Evangelical Christians who traveled to Uganda to speak against "the homosexual agenda"?
2. What is the argument of *The Pink Swastika*, according to Moore?
3. Who is Paul Cameron, and what claims does Moore say that he makes in his self-published studies?

Christians used to go abroad to spread the good news of the saviour. Now a trio of American Evangelicals has been caught sowing the seeds of hatred in Africa.

John Moore, "The Seeds of Hatred," *National Post*, January 12, 2010. Copyright © 2010 CanWest Interactive Inc. and CanWest Publishing Inc. Material reprinted with the express permission of: "National Post Inc."

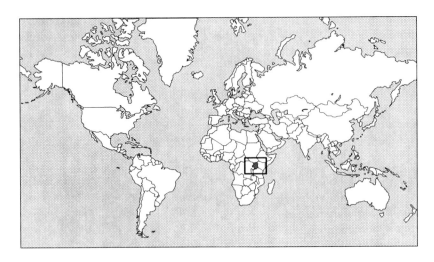

Inspiring Antigay Legislation

In the spring of last year [2009] Scott Lively, Caleb Brundidge and Don Schmierer travelled to Uganda—a country already rife with legislative and social intolerance toward sexual difference—in order to brief thinkers and lawmakers on "the homosexual agenda." They spent three days explaining how "the gay movement is an evil institution whose goal is to defeat the marriage-based society and replace it with a culture of sexual promiscuity." Their meetings inspired a hard-line piece of legislation [proposed in October] calling for gays to be jailed and executed.

Uganda wouldn't be the first country to execute homosexuals. The photograph accompanying this column [not included] shows two teenage boys hanged in Iran four years ago for homosexual activity. Ask yourself if these teens should be playing Wii [a Nintendo game console] in their parents' basement or clerking at a video store rather than lying in their graves. It was only after putting them to death that the theocracy [that controls Iran] hastily juiced up their offence to rape.

To the disgrace of Western Christians the mainstream faith community has been slow in showing even a tepid interest in the Ugandan situation. Evangelical leaders ignored the issue until growing awareness made their silence an embarrassment. Even when their hands were forced, some engaged in the kind of equivocation that suggests that death may be a bit much, but those homos sure have something coming.

Now let's be clear about something: There are those who disapprove of homosexuality and seek to withhold society's sanction of it, while there are others who hate gays the way some hate Jews or ethnics. The problem is an overlapping cohort willing to play Pontius Pilate [the man who authorized Jesus's crucifixion despite personally believing he was not guilty of a capital offence], allowing the haters a greater margin in the service of the common cause of containing homosexuality.

To the disgrace of Western Christians the mainstream faith community has been slow in showing even a tepid interest in the Ugandan situation.

Scientific Nonsense

The scientific flimflammery and intellectual claptrap that Lively, Brundidge and Schmierer preach is derided in the enlightened world, but like a rogue pharmaceutical company they've succeeded in peddling it elsewhere.

Lively is noted for his pseudo-scholarship on homosexual history including the book *The Pink Swastika* in which he maintains that the leadership of the Nazi Party was gay. This, he contends, informed its militarism and inflamed its extremism. Apparently the foundations of [Adolf] Hitler's Germany were largely sound—it's just that the homosexuals had to go gay it up with added killing and mayhem.

Brundidge and Schmierer are part of the "ex-gay" movement which, in spite of ample research establishing that sexual orientation is innate and immutable, works to "cure" homosexuals. The movement's success rate is a dismal affair producing awkward-looking straight couples who dissemble like bad smugglers when asked if they still hanker for gay sex. Prominent ex-homosexuals are often spotted in gay bars but insist that much in the way Mahatma Gandhi used to bed down with virgins to establish his ascetic bona fides, they are simply testing their cure.

The problem for those who don't like homosexuality is that it used to be possible to keep gays and lesbians sidelined through the same collective endeavour that ensured post-emancipation blacks knew their place. Up until the 1970s most gays and lesbians kept their sexuality under wraps. They lived secretive, compartmentalized lives, obscuring their personal activities, likes and dislikes, vacation destinations and partners if they dared have one. Now gays and lesbians are so thoroughly ordinary that few kids think twice about the two women who live across the street and no amount of tut-tutting at the supermarket will get those two men to quit holding hands.

The last trench for those who yearn for the old days of the closet and marginalization is to prop up the crumbling opprobrium against homosexuality by breathing new life into old myths. Lively, Brundidge and Schmierer trade in the homosexual equivalent of the Jewish Blood Libel: The notion that gays recruit, spread disease, molest children and actively conspire against family and society.

Surely the failure of Western Christians to denounce the overt persecution of gays amounts to a mortal sin of omission.

Because the case cannot be established in the real world, the haters rely on the pseudoscience of disgraced psychologist Paul Cameron. Cameron's insidious self-published studies claim the gay male life expectancy is 52 years, based on his culling of newspaper obituaries for the ages of deceased AIDS patients. He maintains that gays and lesbians live miserable solitary lives based on numbers collected in the 1960s when gays and lesbians lived miserable and solitary lives. Cameron has also cooked statistics to prove that gays form the majority of child molesters.

That people of faith traffic in Cameron's junk science is enough of a violation of the commandment against false witness to warrant shame, but surely the failure of Western Christians to denounce the overt persecution of gays amounts to a mortal sin of omission.

It's time for good Christians to stand up and condemn those amongst them who actively or tacitly contribute to the promotion of hatred. Even if that means providing comfort to homosexuals.

By their deeds you will know them.

In Latin America, Homophobia Hinders Anti-AIDS Campaigns

UNAIDS

The Joint United Nations Programme on HIV/AIDS, or UN-AIDS, is the main worldwide advocate for accelerated, comprehensive, and coordinated global action on the AIDS epidemic. In the following viewpoint, the organization notes that Latin American laws do not prosecute homosexuals, but gays still face persecution and violence. The viewpoint states that this is especially dangerous since HIV is prevalent among homosexual men in the region, and homophobia makes it more difficult for these afflicted men to access health services. This, in turn, contributes to the spread of HIV among gay men and other populations.

As you read, consider the following questions:

1. Why does the viewpoint suggest that Brazil and Mexico top the table of violence against men who have sex with men in Latin America?

2. What are the rates of HIV prevalence among MSM in Latin America's main cities, according to this viewpoint?

3. What does this viewpoint say are the goals and plans of the official program "Brazil Without Homophobia"?

UNAIDS, "HIV Prevention Hampered by Homophobia," UNAIDS.org, January 13, 2009. Reproduced by permission.

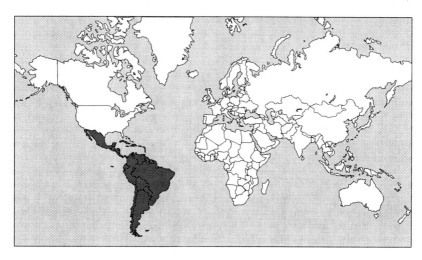

E very two or three days a person is killed in Brazil in vio-
lence connected with his or her sexuality, according to
Brazil's oldest gay rights association, Grupo Gay da Bahia
(GGB). In Mexico, the reported figure is nearly two a week.

Violence Throughout Latin America

Most of the victims are men who have sex with other men
(MSM)—whether they are gays or bisexuals—or transgender
people.

But if Brazil and Mexico top the table of violence against
men who have sex with men in Latin America, this may be
because rights groups there monitor the situation more closely
than elsewhere in Latin America. Much violence simply goes
unreported elsewhere, gay activist organizations say.

"Brazil and Mexico are the only countries which have a
register, which keeps track of the murders. That does not
mean necessarily that there is more violence there," says Arturo Díaz Betancourt of the Mexican National Council for the
Prevention of Discrimination.

It is notable that when the United Nations Special Rappor-
teur [investigator] on extrajudicial killings made an official
mission to Guatemala in 2006 his attention was drawn to a

series of murders of gay and transgender people, and his subsequent report to the Human Rights Council stated, "There has been impunity for murders motivated by hatred towards persons identifying as gay, lesbian, transgender, and transsexual. Credible information suggests that there were at least 35 such murders between 1996 and 2006. Given the lack of official statistics and the likely reticence if not ignorance of victims' family members, there is reason to believe that the actual numbers are significantly higher."

Many Latin American countries boast socially advanced legislation when it comes to defending sexual freedom and orientation. With law reform in Nicaragua and Panama over the past 12 months, there are now no states in Latin America which criminalize homosexual relations, for example.

"There has been impunity for murders motivated by hatred towards persons identifying as gay, lesbian, transgender, and transsexual."

Yet perhaps influenced by a lingering "machismo," prejudice and discrimination continue to flourish, whatever the laws say. Latin America is widely regarded as having a long way to go to successfully counter homophobia, or "fear or hatred of homosexuals."

"There is a real contrast between reality and theory. This is the developing region of the world with the highest number of laws against discrimination based on sexual orientation," says Dr. Ruben Mayorga, UNAIDS [Joint United Nations Programme on HIV/AIDS] Country Coordinator for Argentina, Chile, Paraguay and Uruguay.

Aside from the individual pain homophobic attitudes inflict, the continuing stigma attached to same-sex relations is complicating hugely the task of slowing the spread of HIV in a region where sex between men is a leading mode of HIV transmission, health experts say.

Stigma and homophobia increase the isolation of gays, bisexuals and transgender people making them more reluctant to come forward, be identified and get advice.

"Homophobia represents a threat to public health in Latin America," the Pan American Health Organization affirmed in a report. "This form of stigma and discrimination based on sexual orientation does not just affect the mental and physical health of the homosexual community, but contributes to the spread of the HIV epidemic."

UNAIDS has long campaigned against discrimination whether against those infected by the HIV virus or against a person for his or her sexual orientation.

Sex Between Men Is the Main Source of New HIV Infections

The urgency in Latin America is underlined by official reports on the state of the HIV epidemic in Colombia, Ecuador, Bolivia and Peru where sex between men is acknowledged as being the main source of new HIV infections. HIV prevalence is far higher than in the general population with rates of between 10% and 20% in many [of] Latin America's main cities.

In its 2008 report to the UN General Assembly (UNGASS) on the state of the HIV epidemic, Brazil stated that MSM are 11 times more likely to be HIV positive than the population as a whole.

In parts of Central America, where there is major political and social resistance to recognising the rights of gays, lesbians and transgender people, HIV incidence rates amongst MSM are particularly high.

And the impacts of these high rates of HIV extend beyond men who have sex with men themselves. In Peru, for example, most women who get infected by the virus get it from men who have had sex with other men, according to a Health Ministry study, thus prevention among MSM is crucial for effective prevention of HIV transmission to women.

Estimated HIV/AIDS Prevalence and Deaths Due to AIDS in Latin America, 2007

Country	All People	Living with HIV/AIDS Adult (15–49) Rate %	Deaths Due to AIDS During 2007
Argentina	120,000	0.5	5,400
Belize	3,600	2.1	<200
Bolivia	8,100	0.2	<500
Brazil	730,000	0.6	15,000
Chile	31,000	0.3	<1,000
Colombia	170,000	0.6	9,800
Costa Rica	9,700	0.4	<200
Ecuador	26,000	0.3	1,200
El Salvador	35,000	0.8	1,700
Guatemala	59,000	0.8	3,900
Guyana	13,000	2.5	<1,000
Honduras	28,000	0.7	1,800
Mexico	200,000	0.3	11,000
Nicaragua	7,700	0.2	<500
Panama	20,000	1.0	<1,000
Paraguay	21,000	0.6	<1,000
Peru	76,000	0.5	3,300
Suriname	6,800	2.4	—
Uruguay	10,000	0.6	<500
Venezuela	—	—	—
Total	**1,700,000**	**0.5**	**63,000**

These figures are estimates and are not made with certainty.

TAKEN FROM: Avert, "Latin America Statistics Summary," *Avert*, [2009]. www.avert.org.

Spending on HIV prevention amongst MSM in Latin America is well below what is called for by the extent of the epidemic within that group. On average, less than 10% of the money spent on prevention goes into campaigns aimed specifically at MSM, according to UNAIDS.

In Bolivia, it was estimated in 2005 that fewer than 3% of MSM had access to prevention services, compared with 30% coverage for sex workers.

"All these years, prevention has not been carried out where it needs to be, which is where the epidemic lies," said Diaz. "They have not worked with gays, with trans (gender people), on the contrary there is rejection and deep discrimination," he said, referring to the situation across the region.

In parts of Central America where there is major political and social resistance to recognising the rights of gays, lesbians, and transgender people, HIV incidence rates amongst MSM are particularly high.

The explanation lies in a mix of political, cultural and even religious factors, rights activists and health officials say.

"Politically, MSM is not something to make a lot of noise about. In most countries and by many institutions it is not seen as a political gain," says Mayorga.

Religious groups, whether Roman Catholic or Evangelical, which regard sexual relations between people of the same sex as "sinful," have often strenuously opposed attempts to pay special attention to MSM.

"Governments are highly influenced by religious sectors that mobilise against policies that benefit gays, bisexuals or trans," says Orlando Montoya, who works in Ecuador with ASICAL, an organization promoting the health of gays, other MSM and lesbians in Latin America.

However, it is hard to generalize. Some churches have been at the forefront of outreach to men who have sex with men and many local religious organizations in Latin America have responded to HIV with tolerance and compassion, including among the most marginalized populations.

Latin America Has Been Overlooked

But it is not just a question of country governments not paying due attention to MSM. Latin America has not attracted the level of international investment in stemming HIV epidemics that has been seen in other parts of the world—in Asia and in Africa.

To some extent, the region has been victim of the three "nots" when it comes to receiving international financing for its HIV efforts, Mayorga says. It is "not" very populated, it is "not" very poor and it is "not" a very big epidemic.

Rules covering assistance by the Global Fund to Fight AIDS, Tuberculosis and Malaria, the principal international financing arm against the diseases, have worked against the region because they have tended to exclude middle- and upper-middle-income countries, such as Argentina and Chile.

However, the Fund has recently agreed to study proposals for assistance for programmes in better-off countries facing concentrated epidemics with HIV prevalence rates of over 5% in groups at risk, such as MSM, drug users, transgendered people or sex workers.

In the past four or five years, Brazil and Mexico, and to a more limited extent Argentina and Colombia, have run campaigns against homophobia.

In the face of the persistent evidence of neglect, there are some positive signs in the region that MSM epidemics will be responded to with more adequate measures and policies.

In the past four or five years [before 2009], Brazil and Mexico, and to a more limited extent Argentina and Colombia, have run campaigns against homophobia. These countries, together with others, have also sought to incorporate special MSM action into programmes to contain the spread of HIV.

The official programme "Brazil Without Homophobia" was launched in 2004, with the aim of improving the service given to gays, other MSM and transgender people within state health institutions. It will also scale up coverage and the response to the HIV epidemic within these groups.

Peru has launched a national plan giving priority to prevention programmes for what are defined as "most-affected" groups—which include MSM, sex workers and prisoners. With financing from the Global Fund, the plan aims to extend prevention coverage to at least 25% of MSM and 50% of sex workers.

Similarly, Bolivia has drawn up a national plan to cut HIV infection rates by half by 2015, which includes campaigns to strengthen rights of MSM and transgender people and to combat discrimination and stigma.

Despite these promising developments, Latin America is still a long way from getting its MSM epidemics under control and homophobia and stigma remain significant stumbling blocks to achieving it.

Periodical and Internet Sources Bibliography

The following articles have been selected to supplement the diverse views presented in this chapter.

| Namit Arora | "Homosexuality in India," Countercurrents.org, August 19, 2008. www.countercurrents.org. |

| Andrew Aylward | "Christians Blamed for Anti-Gay Hatred in Uganda," *San Francisco Chronicle*, June 9, 2010. |

| Javier Corrales | "Gays in Latin America: Is the Closet Half Empty?" *Foreign Policy*, February 18, 2009. |

| Javier Corrales | "Latin American Gays: The Post-Left Leftists," *America's Quarterly*, March 19, 2010. http://www.as-coa.org. |

| Michael A. Jones | "The Malaysian Government Thinks That Homosexuality Causes Swine Flu," *Gay Rights*, August 9, 2009. |

| Ephraim Kasozi and Patience Ahimbisibwe | "Uganda: Opposed to Homosexuality—Museveni," allAfrica.com, June 4, 2010. http://allafrica.com. |

| Thomasina Larkin | "Finding Space in Gay Japan," *Japan Times Online*, January 17, 2006. www.japantimes.co.jp. |

| Mark J. McLelland | "Male Homosexuality and Popular Culture in Modern Japan," *Intersections: Gender, History and Culture in the Asian Context*, January 2000. |

| Manoj Mitta and Smriti Singh | "India Decriminalises Gay Sex," *Times of India*, July 3, 2009. |

| Michael Solis | "Uganda's Anti-Homosexuality Bill," *Huffington Post*, February 18, 2010. |

| Peter Williams | "The World's New Gay Rights Battlegrounds," *Foreign Policy*, March 9, 2010. |

GLOBALVIEWPOINTS

CHAPTER 3

Homosexuality and the Law

A Strong Law Against Homosexuality Is Being Proposed in Uganda

Agnes Asiimwe

Agnes Asiimwe is a fellow recipient of the Dag Hammarskjöld Scholarship Fund for Journalists. She is a writer for NTV Uganda, with a special interest in covering African issues. In the following viewpoint, she reports on legislative efforts in Uganda to oppose homosexuality in support of the traditional heterosexual family and on the opposition that stand has received from gay and human rights activists as well as from international political leaders. Religious leaders from both Christian and Muslim faiths support the anti-homosexuality bill, and they say they would prefer to be denied foreign aid from the West than to adopt the policies and lifestyles that are associated with the West as a condition of that aid. Gay and human rights activists fear that the bill will keep gay people from seeking help related to AIDS.

As you read, consider the following questions:

1. Who is Yoweri Museveni, and what is his position on the anti-homosexuality bill?

Agnes Asiimwe, "Anti-Gay Bill on Course; David Bahati, the Author of Uganda's Anti-Gay Bill Aiming to Criminalise Homosexuality in the Country, Says the Bill Is Still on Course Despite a Thunderous International Outcry Against It," *New African*, February 2010, p. 42. Reprinted with permission.

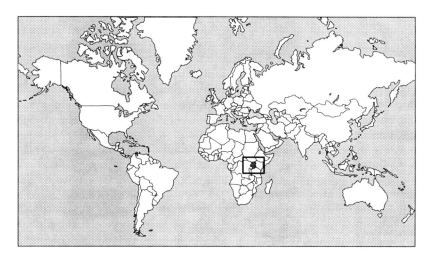

2. For what political issues, aside from issues of religion and family, does Martin Ssempa say that the bill has implications?

3. Who are Paul Kagaba and Val Kalende, and what are their positions on the anti-homosexuality bill?

Uganda's new controversial antigay bill proposes a seven-year jail term for homosexuals and a death penalty for those convicted of aggravated homosexuality, which is defined as sex with a minor or a disabled person where the offender is HIV positive.

The author of the bill, David Bahati, MP [member of Parliament] for Ndorwa West constituency, who has since October 2009 been on the receiving end of increasing outrage by gay and human rights activists worldwide, and even claims to be getting death threats, remains defiant. His bill, he says, is meant to protect "the traditional African heterosexual family".

World leaders, including President Barack Obama, and Prime Minister Gordon Brown of the UK [United Kingdom], have spoken out against the proposed legislation. Sweden and Canada have threatened to cut aid to Uganda if the bill is passed. America has also said Uganda's beneficiary status under the African Growth and Opportunity Act (AGOA) will be revoked if the bill goes ahead.

But Martin Ssempa, an outspoken antigay pastor in Uganda, has sneered at the threats: "If our selling of our cotton to America means that we get sodomy in exchange, then we don't need that business."

Ugandan religious leaders from the Christian, Pentecostal and Muslim faiths are fully behind the bill and have called on Western leaders to "back off". The pastors and Muslim clerics have called on their congregations to vote out any parliamentarian who does not support the bill. They have in the past organised several antigay demonstrations in Kampala. "Our donor partners have put a lot of pressure on our government, disrespectfully interfering in our democratic process of lawmaking," said Bahati. President Yoweri Museveni, himself not so friendly to homosexuality, has, in a surprising change of heart, asked the MPs behind the bill to "go slow".

World leaders, including President Barack Obama, and Prime Minister Gordon Brown of the UK, have spoken out against the proposed legislation.

"This is a foreign policy issue and we have to discuss it in a manner that does not compromise our principles but also takes care of our foreign policy interests," Museveni told a gathering of the National Executive Committee of his ruling NRM [National Resistance Movement] party, as MPs shouted: "No, no, no!"

Museveni told them about a gay rally in New York that garnered 300,000 homosexuals. "Who of you, MPs, has ever had a rally of 300,000 people, other than me?" Museveni asked. "Even for me, it is not often that I get those numbers." The MPs murmured in disagreement.

Pastor Martin Ssempa has already announced that he will organise a similar rally. "We'll mobilise more than 300,000 people and we'll tell the president to send the pictures to Hillary Clinton and Obama." Ssempa agrees that the issue has foreign policy implications, "but also national sovereignty implications."

The supporters of the bill claim that homosexuals are recruiting, especially in single-sex schools.

"No government should put sodomy as their foreign policy priority," Ssempa said. "If giving us mosquito nets and anti-AIDS drugs involves us doing sodomy, we would rather die in dignity because we have cherished our values and cultures for hundreds of years."

The supporters of the bill claim that homosexuals are recruiting, especially in single-sex schools. Several young men have appeared claiming they were recruited and lured into homosexuality. The antigay advocates have accused international organisations of fanning the gay propaganda. One such "reformed homosexual", Paul Kagaba, pointed out Western-controlled NGOs [nongovernmental organisations].

In contrast, human rights activists have accused the antigay agitators of wanting to kill in God's name. "The effect of this legislation will demonise homosexuality even further, intensify stigma and drive gay men and women underground, and diminish prospects of counselling and testing to establish HIV status," said Val Kalende, who recently went public about her lesbian status.

However, there are unconfirmed reports that Museveni has assured the US assistant secretary of state for African affairs, Johnnie Carson, that he will veto the law if it sails through Parliament.

Nigeria's Laws Against Homosexuality Violate Human Rights

Human Rights Watch

Human Rights Watch (HRW) is a nongovernmental organization that conducts human rights research and advocacy. In the following viewpoint, the organization argues that a proposed Nigerian law banning same-sex marriage would allow draconian invasion of privacy, threatening all Nigerians. HRW also maintains that the law would make fighting HIV/AIDS more difficult by forcing some of the populations infected with the disease underground. The viewpoint states that the law violates international human rights standards and should not be passed.

As you read, consider the following questions:

1. According to the viewpoint, how is HIV most often spread in Nigeria?
2. The five-year sentence for those who "abet" a same-sex relationship could be used to punish which individuals or groups, according to the viewpoint?
3. What did the 2006 bill discussed in this viewpoint seek to criminalize?

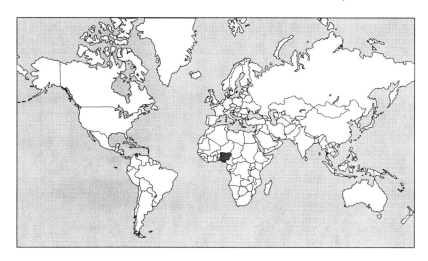

(New York)—A bill before Nigeria's National Assembly to ban "same gender marriage" would expand Nigeria's already draconian punishments for homosexual conduct and threaten all Nigerians' rights to privacy, free expression, and association, Human Rights Watch said today.

In a letter to President Umaru Yar'Adua, leaders of the House of Representatives and Senate, the Nigerian National Human Rights Commission, and other national, regional, and international bodies, the group urged legislators and the president to reject the bill. The letter urged the country's leaders to combat an environment of stigma and violence against lesbian, gay, bisexual, and transgender (LGBT) Nigerians.

On January 15, 2009, the Nigerian House of Representatives voted favorably on the second reading of a bill "to prohibit marriage between persons of the same gender." The bill would punish people of the same sex who live together "as husband and wife or for other purposes of same-sexual relationship" with up to three years of imprisonment. Anyone who "witnesses, abet[s] and aids" such a relationship could be imprisoned for up to five years.

"This bill masquerades as a law on marriage, but in fact it violates the privacy of anyone even suspected of an intimate relationship with a person of the same sex," said Georgette Gagnon, Africa director at Human Rights Watch. "It also threatens basic freedoms by punishing human rights defenders who speak out for unpopular causes."

The House of Representatives referred the bill to its committees on Human Rights, Justice, and Women Affairs, which will hold a joint public hearing on it. If the House approves the bill on a third reading, it must then be approved by the Senate and President Yar'Adua.

"This bill [outlawing same-sex partnerships] masquerades as a law on marriage, but in fact it violates the privacy of anyone even suspected of an intimate relationship with a person of the same sex."

Members of the House of Representatives reportedly justified the bill by citing links between "sodomy" and HIV and AIDS, making clear that they see the marriage ban as a deterrent to homosexual conduct, though research shows that HIV is most often spread through heterosexual conduct in Nigeria. Article 214 of the Nigerian Criminal Code Act already provides up to 14 years of imprisonment for anyone who "has carnal knowledge of any person against the order of nature." As Human Rights Watch documented in a December 2008 report, this law is a Victorian-era provision that remained after the end of British colonial rule.

The proposed law contravenes several provisions of regional and international human rights standards. Article 2 of the African Charter on Human and Peoples' Rights promises every individual equal entitlement to rights and freedoms without distinction of any kind; article 3 of the charter guarantees all individuals equality before the law; and article 26 states that: "Every individual shall have the duty to respect and consider his fellow beings without discrimination and to maintain relations aimed at promoting, safeguarding and reinforcing mutual respect and tolerance."

The United Nations Human Rights Committee, which authoritatively interprets the International Covenant on Civil and Political Rights (ICCPR) and evaluates states' compliance with its provisions, found in the 1994 case of *Toonen v. Australia* that laws criminalizing consensual, adult homosexual conduct violate the covenant's protections for privacy and against discrimination. Nigeria acceded to the covenant without reservations in 1993.

In its letter, Human Rights Watch pointed to grave human rights issues raised by the proposed law:

- The evident intent of the new bill is to extend the already existing penalties for homosexual conduct.

- Criminalizing "living together as husband and wife" further expands these punishments. They would no longer be limited to sexual acts between people of the same sex, but would potentially include mere cohabitation or any suspected "intimate relationship" between members of the same sex. Far less evidence would be needed for conviction, and prejudice and suspicion would be a basis for arrests. This threatens all Nigerians' right to private life.

- The proposed five-year sentence for those who "abet" a same-sex relationship is greater than the punishment stipulated in the bill for those who enter into a "same-gender marriage." This provision could be used to punish anyone who gives any help or advice to a suspected "same-gender" couple—anyone who rents them an apartment, tells them their rights, or approves of their relationships. Advocates, civil society organizations, and human rights defenders would be ready targets.

- Under the bill's provisions, anyone—whether Nigerian or foreign—who enters into a "same-gender marriage," or simply has a "same-gender relationship" in another country and wishes to continue it in Nigeria, could be subject to criminal penalties when they set foot on Nigerian soil. This provides the state with even broader powers to invade people's privacy.

Far less evidence would be needed for conviction, and prejudice and suspicion would be a basis for arrests. This threatens all Nigerians' right to private life.

Similar concerns were raised in a joint public statement issued by Amnesty International and Nigerian nongovernmental organizations.

In 2006, Nigeria's minister of justice proposed a similar bill, seeking to criminalize not only same-sex unions but also public advocacy and associations supporting the rights of lesbian and gay people. Sixteen human rights groups—from Nigeria, across Africa, and around the world—had condemned the bill for violating the freedoms of expression, association, and assembly guaranteed by international law as well as the African Charter on Human and Peoples' Rights, and for further jeopardizing the fight against the HIV and AIDS epidemic in the country. That legislation failed to come to a vote in the National Assembly.

Nigeria has the world's third-largest population of people living with AIDS. Data collected by international health organizations suggest that 80 percent of HIV infections in Nigeria result from heterosexual sex, which discredits the equation between "sodomy" and AIDS as drawn by the members of the House of Representatives. The proposed bill would further hinder HIV and AIDS education and prevention efforts in the country by driving some groups affected by the epidemic further underground for fear of violence. In July 2008, the UN-

AIDS (Joint United Nations Programme on HIV/AIDS) country report on Nigeria recognized that criminalization of vulnerable populations, including men who have sex with men, makes HIV and AIDS prevention and treatment efforts less accessible to these populations.

The proposed bill would further hinder HIV and AIDS education and prevention efforts in the country by driving some groups affected by the epidemic further underground for fear of violence.

Violence against LGBT people is frequent in Nigeria. In September 2008, several national newspapers published articles criticizing a Christian church in Lagos that ministers to LGBT people: The articles included names, addresses, and photographs of members of the congregation and the church's pastor. Police harassment and threats forced the church to shut down and the pastor to flee the country. Some members of the congregation lost their jobs and homes and had to go into hiding, and several of them continue to be under threat of physical harm and harassment.

"This legislation would allow the state to invade people's homes and bedrooms and investigate their private lives, and it would criminalize the work of human rights defenders," said Gagnon. "It is not a ban on marriage, but an assault on basic rights."

In Iran, Homosexuals Are Not Forced to Become Transsexuals

Hossein Derakhshan

Hossein Derakhshan is an Iranian-born blogger, journalist, and Internet activist. In the following viewpoint, he argues that in Iran homosexuals are not forced to become transsexuals, as the documentary film Be Like Others *by Tanaz Eshaghian appears to portray. On the contrary, he says Iranian culture does not make clear distinctions between homosexual and heterosexual. Homosexuals are not persecuted, but are instead tolerated. Derakhshan suggests that the film distorted the truth in order to promote an anti-Iranian agenda.*

As you read, consider the following questions:

1. According to Derakhshan, what did Ahmadinejad say in a speech at Columbia University?

2. How does Derakhshan say that Eshaghian mistranslated the words of a young cleric who defends sex-change operations?

3. What names does Derakhshan say were missing from the BBC credits of Eshaghian's documentary?

Hossein Derakhshan, "Transsexuals in Iran: Another Anti-Iranian Propaganda That Doesn't Exactly Work as It Should," Iranian.com, February 29, 2008. Reproduced by permission.

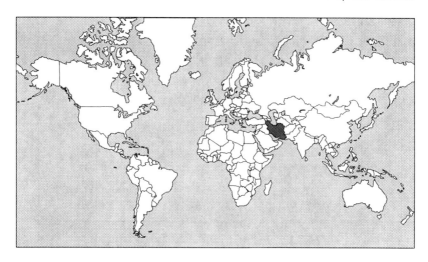

If you are a Jewish Iranian, living in the U.S. from the age of 6, it is very likely you don't like [Iranian President Mahmoud] Ahmadinejad [who is well known for his anti-Semitic statements]. So of course you would like to show how you hate him and how he is such a liar and how evil the entire government he represents is, in any way you can.

Dishonest and Unfair

So you decide to attack one of the only positive angles Iran has been reported: Sex change. And why not connect it to Ahmadinejad's speech in your city's university, Columbia, [in 2007] where he said in Iran homosexuality doesn't exist the same way it does in the U.S. (We all know the united Republican/Democrat anti-Iran front translated that to a denial of homosexuals in Iran.)

Tanaz Eshaghian's *Be Like Others* (or *Transsexual in Iran,* as BBC titled it) is a well-made documentary, but it is dishonest and unfair. It basically [says] being gay in Iran is so hard that [it] forces gay men to go through the brutal process of sex change. So even though the Islamic Republic [of Iran] looks surprisingly cool with transsexuality on the surface, it is actually killing scores of gay men by separating them from their family, forcing them into a constant struggle of identity, inflicting physical and psychological pain on them—and turning them into prostitutes, in the end.

But this is not exactly what every viewer would see in the film. They might ask, for instance, if being gay is so hard, how come Ali (Anoush's boyfriend) doesn't feel marginalized, isolated, or even under any kind of pressure?

Ali's character . . . is a living evidence of how homosexuality exists in Iran and how and why it is tolerated.

Ali likes Anoush even before Anoush does the sex-change operation and while he still has male sexual organs. So if Iran is so cruel to homosexuals and hangs them, how come Ali is still not only walking, but working as a hairdresser and even is so comfortable with his name, face and identity [that he lets them] be revealed by the film?

Ali's character, in my mind, is the most important one in the film and he is the one that undoes the main message of the film. He is a living evidence of how homosexuality exists in Iran and how and why it is tolerated, and Eshaghian fails to bring it into her core message of the film.

Straight and Gay Are Blurred

He [Ali's character] shows how homosexuality, as a social phenomenon, doesn't exist in Iran because the lines between being straight and gay have historically been blurred in the Iranian culture. Sexuality has never been forced into strict categories in Iran and this could be quite related to what Judith Butler [a philosopher and critic who claims gender is fluid] argues in her work.

But the film is also dishonest in details. The most important part, which is also central to the core of the message, is when she shamelessly mistranslates the young cleric who defends sex-change operations. He says transsexuality has noth-

Transsexuality Allows for a Brand New Discourse

"People would be coming in to get the operation and they'd still say they weren't gay. . . . They see it as a behavior that someone is choosing to become willfully. . . . Whereas with transsexuality, they've created a different discourse around it. It's out of their control, it's kind of like cancer, it's medical so they can't be judged for it."

Kyle Buchanan,
"Director Tanaz Eshaghian on Her Gay Iranian Transsexual Doc
Be Like Others," *Movieline.com, June 18, 2009. www.movieline.com.*

ing to do with homosexuality which is "immoral and irreligious." But guess how it is translated by Eshaghian to twist his logic: "something unnatural and against religion." Wow!

The lines between being straight and gay have historically been blurred in the Iranian culture.

I don't want to get into the list of funders and producers of the film. But I can't resist the temptation of raising two questions. Especially given the continuous anti-Iran propaganda the BBC Two [a British television station] has produced and showed in the past few years.

a) Why Alexandra Kerry's name (Yes, [Democratic senator] John Kerry's daughter), as a co-producer is missing from the BBC credits?

b) Why the name of another co-producer, Ilan Ziv, an Israeli filmmaker and producer with such films as *Human Weapon* (on the history of suicide bombing traced back to Iran) and *People Power* (on "nonviolent revolutions around the world" with insight from Gene Sharp, "a leading expert on nonviolent struggles") is also removed from the BBC credits?

In Canada, Hate Crime Laws Aid Gays and Police

Gerald Bellett

Gerald Bellett is a journalist whose work has appeared in the Vancouver Sun. In the following viewpoint, he reports that police and gay organizations want to use hate crime laws to prosecute a man accused of attacking a homosexual man in Vancouver. If the assault is prosecuted as a hate crime, Bellett notes, the sentencing will be more severe. Bellett says that police and gay organizations believe that enforcing hate crime laws will help to highlight the seriousness of the offense.

As you read, consider the following questions:

1. Who was Aaron Webster, according to Brian Yuen?
2. What happened to Spencer Herbert just hours before the attack on Smith?
3. Why was the assault on Smith initially dealt with in community court, according to the viewpoint?

Members of Vancouver's gay community have joined Vancouver police in urging that hate crime provisions of the Criminal Code be applied in what is alleged to have been an unprovoked attack on a gay man preceded by antigay insults.

Gerald Bellett, "Gay Community Joins Police in Urging Hate Crime Charges," *Vancouver Sun*, September 30, 2008. Material reprinted with the express permission of: "Pacific Newspaper Group Inc.," a Postmedia Network Partnership.

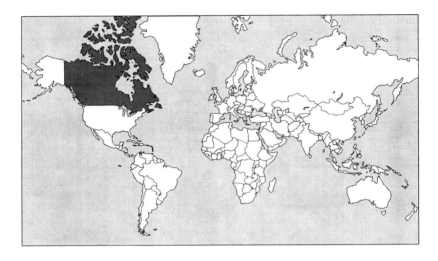

Hate Crimes Carry Heavier Penalties

Michael Kandola, 20, of Vancouver, appeared in Vancouver Downtown Community Court Monday [in September 2008] accused of assaulting Jordan Smith, 27, of White Rock.

Smith was knocked unconscious and had his jaw broken in three places following a confrontation with a group of males shortly after midnight Saturday on Davie Street.

However, Crown counsel Andrew Cochrane told Judge David Pendleton that the assault "was not a community court matter" and Kandola was ordered to appear in provincial court today.

Cochrane said information was being prepared concerning new charges against Kandola that would have to be dealt with in provincial court.

The assault charge could be upgraded to assault causing bodily harm or the more serious offence, aggravated assault.

Stan Lowe, a spokesman with the attorney-general's ministry, said Monday that prosecutors are awaiting details from the Vancouver police regarding the extent of Smith's injuries.

"We are waiting for medical evidence so that we can assess whether the charges should be upgraded from simple assault," said Lowe.

Vancouver police have said the assault against Smith should be dealt with as a hate crime at sentencing if a conviction is obtained.

Changes to the Criminal Code allow a judge to impose heavier penalties if there is evidence that an offence was motivated by hatred based on such things as race, religion or sexual orientation.

Kandola, who was arrested by police after the assault, then released, was represented by Richmond lawyer Danny Markovitz.

As Kandola—a short, stocky man—left the court, he was mobbed by camera operators and reporters shouting questions. He kept his head down, walked quickly to a waiting car and jumped in before it sped away.

Changes to the Criminal Code allow a judge to impose heavier penalties if there is evidence that an offence was motivated by hatred based on such things as race, religion or sexual orientation.

Antigay Obscenities and Assault

The assault is alleged to have occurred when Smith was walking and holding hands with a male friend in the 900-block Davie.

Smith said they were followed by four or five males who began yelling antigay obscenities. One of the group got in front of him and another punched him in the side of the face.

He said he didn't see the punch coming and the next thing he remembers is waking up in hospital. After surgery, which was to take place Monday, he expects his jaw will be wired shut for six weeks.

Vancouver lawyer Brian Yuen, co-chair of Vancouver's Gay and Lesbian Business Association, said he hopes the assault is deemed a hate crime.

"We had an awful incident in 2001 when Aaron Webster was beaten to death by four individuals but the attackers in that case were not dealt with under hate crime laws," he said.

(Webster died in November 2001 after being attacked by a group of males in Stanley Park in an area known to be frequented by gay males.)

"Things like this threaten the health, welfare and safety of the [gay] community and I hope the criminal case will proceed as a hate crime. This is the sort of thing that makes people live in fear and in this day and age that shouldn't happen."

"This kind of thing could easily destroy a life or a career," he added. "I can't say how often it occurs in the community as not everything is reported, but we do see a lot of less serious offences such as name-calling."

Spencer Herbert, a Vancouver park board commissioner and provincial NDP [New Democratic Party] candidate in Vancouver-Burrard, said he and his partner had a homophobic slur yelled at them from a car as they walked by English Bay just hours before the attack on Smith.

Herbert said such instances happen in the West End with "fair frequency" and he believes they've increased in the last year.

[A local public figure] said education is key to combating homophobia, but he'd also like to see a provincial hotline to report gay bashing, since victims can be reluctant to go public after an attack.

"Friends have been physically chased, shoved, been sworn at," Herbert said.

"I think sometimes people see this as a destination where they can come and unleash their hate," he said. "Quite often the people are drunk, maybe they've come down to party and [are] looking to pick a fight after a night at the bar."

He said education is key to combating homophobia, but he'd also like to see a provincial hotline to report gay bashing, since victims can be reluctant to go public after an attack.

"It's just a real wake-up call," he said of the attack on Smith. "I think people have grown complacent a bit and seem to think that we've made all this progress. But I still wouldn't want to be a kid in high school coming out [that is, telling friends and family he or she is gay]."

Unsafe in Their Own Neighbourhoods

Smith was assaulted less than a block away from the law office of barbara findlay, who describes herself as a lesbian feminist lawyer, and does not use capital letters in her name.

"As a lesbian it makes me feel unsafe in my own neighbourhood. It means that not one of us is safe," findlay said Monday.

"In a time when we are constitutionally protected by Canadian society, that anyone should feel they have permission to attack us physically and get away with it, is stunning," she said.

It would be the first time in [British Columbia] that the Criminal Code's hate crime provisions are used against someone involved in gay bashing.

She, too, wants the court to regard the incident as a hate crime.

If there is a conviction and the judge finds the assault was provoked by sexual orientation, it would be the first time in B.C. [British Columbia, the province where Vancouver is located] that the Criminal Code's hate crime provisions are used against someone involved in gay bashing, she said.

"I can't think of any other cases. I know it was not used in the Aaron Webster prosecution. But if it is accepted and there is a conviction I look forward to seeing how it increases sentencing," said findlay.

Canadian Hate Crimes, 2006

Type of Motivation	Violent Crime		Property Crime		Other Crime		Total	
	Number	%	Number	%	Number	%	Number	%
Race/ethnicity								
Black	90	37.8	122	51.3	26	10.9	238	100.0
South Asian	25	37.9	36	54.5	5	7.6	66	100.0
Arab/West Asian	30	49.2	24	39.3	7	11.5	61	100.0
East/Southeast Asian	12	48.0	9	36.0	4	16.0	25	100.0
Caucasian	11	45.8	11	45.8	2	8.3	24	100.0
Aboriginal	8	50.0	6	37.5	2	12.5	16	100.0
Multiple races/ethnicities	6	16.2	29	78.4	2	5.4	37	100.0
Other	10	34.5	14	48.3	5	17.2	29	100.0
Unknown	1	16.7	5	83.3	0	0.0	6	100.0
Total	**193**	**38.4**	**256**	**51.0**	**53**	**10.6**	**502**	**100.0**
Religion								
Jewish	32	23.4	96	70.1	9	6.6	137	100.0
Muslim (Islam)	19	41.3	19	41.3	8	17.4	46	100.0
Catholic	1	7.7	7	53.8	5	38.5	13	100.0

continued

Canadian Hate Crimes, 2006 [CONTINUED]

Type of Motivation	Violent Crime		Property Crime		Other crime		Total	
	Number	%	Number	%	Number	%	Number	%
Other	6	30.0	11	55.0	3	15.0	20	100.0
Unknown	0	0.0	4	100.0	0	0.0	4	100.0
Total	**58**	**26.4**	**137**	**62.3**	**25**	**11.4**	**220**	**100.0**
Sexual orientation								
Other	45	56.3	29	36.3	6	7.5	80	100.0
Unknown	26	38.2	27	39.7	15	22.1	68	100.0
Total	**327**	**36.7**	**460**	**51.6**	**105**	**11.8**	**892**	**100.0**

TAKEN FROM: Statistics Canada, "Police-Reported Hate Crimes by Type of Motivation and Crime Category," August 13, 2009. www.statcan.gc.ca.

Findlay said while Saturday's incident will make the community fearful and more "wary and careful," it will not "make us become invisible."

"I think this community turned a corner with the Aaron Webster murder. It galvanized us and we refused to be afraid and go back into the closet," she said.

Vancouver police spokesman Const. [Constable] Tim Fanning said such assaults are rare.

"For the most part, people who are openly gay and showing affection feel comfortable and that reflects well on the city. What happened this weekend is a rare event," Fanning said.

"We had an incident about six months ago when items were thrown at a gay man in the West End that was a concern to us as it might have been a hate crime, but a follow-up investigation proved it not to be so," said Fanning.

As for why the weekend incident was dealt with in community court, Lowe said that had to do with the original charge being assault committed in the downtown area of Vancouver that falls under the jurisdiction of the Vancouver Downtown Community Court.

"It went there because of the location of the incident but we proceeded by way of indictment so it had to move up to the provincial court. The community court only deals with summary matters," he said

Vancouver's Downtown Community Court has been set up to deal with repeat offenders, many of whom suffer from mental illness or drug addiction or both. They are frequently homeless or lacking in job skills and social supports.

The court uses a variety of methods to deal with offenders, including ordering them into drug or alcohol treatment or counselling and seeks to deal with the underlying causes of criminal behaviour rather than sentencing them to jail.

In the United States, Hate Crime Laws Protecting Homosexuals Violate Freedom of Speech

Jerry A. Kane

Jerry A. Kane is a technical writer, editor, adjunct professor, and journalist whose commentaries have appeared on websites such as World Net Daily *and* American Thinker. *In the following viewpoint, he asserts that evidence from Europe and Canada shows that hate crime laws are inequitable, arguing that they give minorities rights under the law that are denied to majority groups. Kane also contends that the laws restrict freedom of speech by making it illegal to criticize homosexuals. He concludes that hate crime laws are unconstitutional and should not be passed in the United States.*

As you read, consider the following questions:

1. According to Kane, what law if passed will make homosexuals a federally protected class?

2. Why does Kane say that the police in Britain asked the Crown Prosecution Service to bring charges against the makers of the film *Undercover Mosque?*

Jerry A. Kane, "Making Free Speech a Hate Crime," American Daughter Media Center, May 7, 2009. Reproduced by permission of the author.

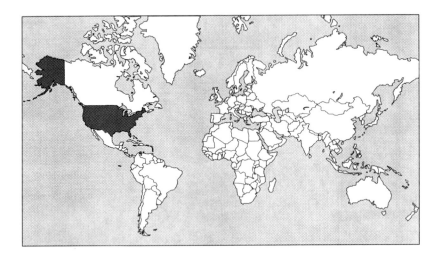

3. In May 2006, why did a Belgium man file a complaint with the Centre for Equal Opportunities and Opposition to Racism, and what was the agency director's decision, according to Kane?

The hate crime bill that passed the U.S. House of Representatives April 29 [2009] is an attempt by Democratic Socialists and Progressives to silence dissent against alternative lifestyles. Their incessant iconoclastic attacks on once-established values and morality have nearly eroded this nation's spiritual and cultural legacy. Instituting same-sex marriage and prosecuting hate speech will complete the process and shatter the remaining hopes for cultural regeneration and tear down the last vestiges of the country's Judeo-Christian ethic.

Suppressing Politically Incorrect Views

In America's brave new post-modern multi-culture, homosexual and transgender people will become a federally protected class under the Local Law Enforcement Hate Crimes Prevention Act of 2009. . . . Under this act, anyone who publicly opposes the practice of homosexuality or any of the 30 other sexual orientations as designated by the American Psychiatric Association (APA) could be charged with expressing "hateful words" and convicted of a "hate crime."

Under the guise of tolerance, Canada and European countries have implemented hate crimes legislation to suppress expressions that conflict with public opinion or do not conform to politically correct policies, i.e., the views of the state are the views of the people. Only designated groups and minorities belong to the protected classes. The majority of Canadians and Europeans are not free to express politically incorrect religious beliefs, moral convictions, and political ideas publicly for fear they may enrage members in the protected classes.

Britain's hate crimes legislation should be renamed the Islam Protection Act. In January 2007, British television aired *Undercover Mosque*, a documentary about Islamic extremism in Britain. The documentary was based on a 12-month secret investigation into mosques throughout the nation. In the footage, Muslim preachers exhort followers to prepare for jihad [Islamic holy war], incite violence against non-Muslims, urge followers to reject British laws, and praise the Taliban [a Muslim fundamentalist insurgent group in Afghanistan] for killing a British soldier.

Canada and European countries have implemented hate crimes legislation to suppress expressions that . . . do not conform to politically correct policies.

Leaders in the Muslim community complained the film was discriminatory and intimidating, so the police requested that the Crown Prosecution Service (CPS) prosecute the filmmakers for "stirring up racial hatred." By ignoring facts and what had actually happened, the police and CPS found common ground with the film's detractors—that is to say, they agreed the Islamic clerics were harmless victims whose sermons were "taken out of context" and condemned the filmmakers for religious bigotry and inciting racial hatred. Alas, clairvoyance has supplanted the blindfolded matron, Lady Justice.

Hate crime laws are rarely enforced when slurs, insults, invectives, and ridicule are hurled at members in the majority group.

No Equality Under Law

Hate crimes legislation allows a country's legal system to disregard any notion of equality under the law and apply it unequally and selectively, which means that some citizens are harassed, prosecuted, and convicted, while others are not. In Canada and European countries, hate crime prosecutions of heterosexuals, non-Muslims, or non-Socialists exceed those of homosexuals, Muslims, and Socialists.

Hate crime laws are rarely enforced when slurs, insults, invectives, and ridicule are hurled at members in the majority group. For example, in May 2006, a Belgium man filed a complaint with the police against the Centre for Equal Opportunities and Opposition to Racism because he was offended by the agency's use of the words "Dirty Heterosexual" in its postcard distribution campaign. The agency director said that stigmatizing or discriminating against majorities is "not real discrimination" and dismissed the man's objections with "laughter" saying, "Discrimination is something that by definition affects minorities."

Hate crime laws establish a preferential justice system and create a double standard in the legal system that fosters distrust, conflict, and intolerance in a society. Such laws suggest that members of a minority group deserve a higher level of justice than those of the majority, which makes members of the minority group more important and morally superior. In Austria, it's not considered degrading to Christians if Jesus is

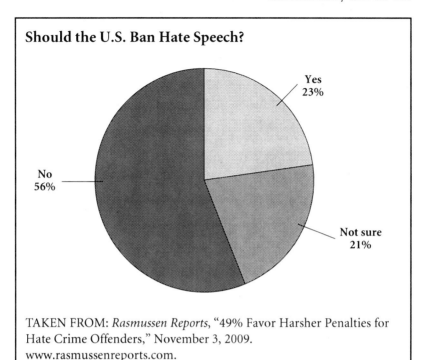

Should the U.S. Ban Hate Speech?

Yes
23%

No
56%

Not sure
21%

TAKEN FROM: *Rasmussen Reports*, "49% Favor Harsher Penalties for Hate Crime Offenders," November 3, 2009. www.rasmussenreports.com.

portrayed in homosexual acts with his apostles, but it is degrading to Muslims if the historical fact that Muhammad married a six-year-old girl is mentioned.

Polemicists who denounce homosexuality and same-sex marriage are no less entitled to their opinions than the apologists who promote them.

In Britain, a 69-year-old evangelical was prosecuted for displaying a protest sign with the words "Stop Immorality. Stop Homosexuality. Stop Lesbianism." Objecting to his peaceful protest, hecklers knocked him down, threw dirt on him, poured water over his head, and tried to take his placard. The police came and arrested the protester, but did nothing to those who assaulted him.

The magistrates' court ruled that the words on the placard could be harassing, alarming, and distressful for homosexuals who may find the words threatening, abusive, or insulting. Consequently, the evangelical protester was fined and ordered to pay court costs for displaying words that might offend the delicate sensibilities of a protected class member, but the criminal actions of the hecklers who assaulted him were disregarded and left unpunished.

Criminalizing Speech

Fears that hate crime laws will eventually lead to criminalizing speech are not unfounded. In 2001 [in Canada], a Saskatchewan resident published an ad in a local newspaper that consisted of a few Bible verses and an illustration of two stickman figures holding hands inside a circle with a line though it. The Saskatchewan Human Rights Tribunal ordered the resident and newspaper to pay $4,500 to three homosexuals who had been traumatized and scarred for life by the stickman illustration.

Polemicists who denounce homosexuality and same-sex marriage are no less entitled to their opinions than the apologists who promote them. What has happened to religious freedom and freedom of conscience in Canada and Europe as the result of implementing hate crime laws is clear. Make no mistake, if the recently passed hate crime bill becomes law in the United States, freedom of speech will be sacrificed to protect particular classes from criticism and all forms of upset, making condemnation of homosexuality illegal.

Hate crime laws violate the fundamental notion that man's natural equality entitles him to impartial justice, which is the underlying principle of the Constitution and Bill of Rights. How ironic the counterculture Left that chanted in the 1960s, "I may disapprove of what you say, but I will defend to the death your right to say it," now fights to enslave all Americans to the will of a totalitarian bureaucracy.

The Mexican Government Launches an Ad Campaign Against Homophobia

Monica Campbell

Monica Campbell was a journalist based in Mexico City from 2002 to 2008, reporting on immigration, politics, and drug violence. She was a 2009–2010 Nieman Fellow at Harvard, and is now a freelance journalist based in New York. In the following viewpoint, she reports on Mexico's efforts to stop the spread of AIDS. In 2001, a constitutional amendment against discrimination, including that based on sexuality, became law. In 2003, federal agencies had to fund tolerance campaigns. Conservative Catholic groups oppose the use of tax funds to validate a way of life that they consider wayward and that increases the risk of AIDS. Campaign supporters hope that building tolerance for homosexuals will encourage them to get tested and improve doctors' treatment of AIDS.

As you read, consider the following questions:

1. What other Latin American country has used federal funds to combat public sentiment against homosexuality?

2. What group is most at risk for the spread of AIDS in Mexico?

Monica Campbell, "Mexico Tackles Discrimination to Fight Aids: The Government Has Launched an Ad Campaign Against Homophobia, but Some Critics Oppose Using Tax Dollars," *Christian Science Monitor*, June 9, 2005. Reprinted with permission from the author and *Christian Science Monitor*, www.csmonitor.com.

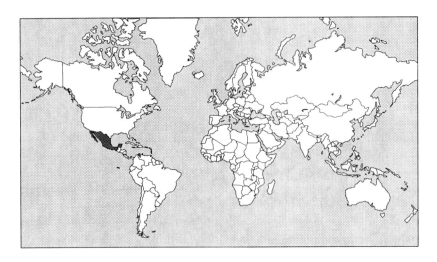

3. What percentage of Mexican people in a survey said they would not share a house with an HIV-positive person?

Mexico City—The Mexican government has launched its first ever anti-homophobia campaign to encourage people to get tested for the AIDS virus.

In one radio ad, a mother preparing dinner for her son and his date, whom he is bringing home for the first time, says: "You look so in love, my son. So what's your date's name?"

"Oscar," her son says.

The narrator then conveys that equality begins with accepting people's differences.

The campaign, currently airing in 19 cities and set to go nationwide this month [June 2005], is ruffling feathers in this Catholic country, with much of the criticism focused on using public funds to pay for the ads. But AIDS continues to spread here, and the government hopes that destigmatizing homosexuality will enable more people to come forward and get help.

The commercials stem from a 2001 constitutional amendment signed by President Vicente Fox, which outlawed discrimination, including bias based on sexuality. In 2003, federal agencies were required to fund tolerance campaigns. After Brazil, Mexico is the second Latin American country to use federal funds to tackle homophobia. Health workers and AIDS activists applaud Mr. Fox for green-lighting the effort.

AIDS continues to spread here, and the government hopes that destigmatizing homosexuality will enable more people to come forward and get help.

"Fox gave this campaign some legs, despite his government's ultraconservative image," says Alejandro Brito, a long-time AIDS activist and director of *Letra S*, a newspaper supplement here that focuses on sexual diversity. "It's a positive step. For the first time, the government is recognizing that religious concerns should not interfere with a public-health problem."

Conservative Catholic groups like the National Unity of Parents and Pro-Life, a politically connected antiabortion organization, oppose the anti-homophobia campaign. "We are not saying homosexuals should be discriminated against," says Guillermo Bustamante, the head of National Unity, in an interview. "But this is work for nongovernmental groups, not something our taxes should pay for. Why should we fund a mainstream media campaign that validates wayward tendencies and sexual activity that puts people most at risk of getting AIDS?"

National Unity has produced its own radio spots. One ad features a daughter telling her mother she is attracted to women. The mother says she appreciates her daughter's openness and pledges to help her from acting out "tendencies that could affect her gravely."

So far, the government has decided not to run the National Unity ads.

Mexico's AIDS numbers are not growing at the same rate as other parts of Latin America, namely in Central America and the Caribbean. But not unlike the situation in the United States, Mexican health officials are struggling to control the spread of AIDS among the country's most vulnerable group: men, generally between 25 and 40 years old.

At the end of 2004, the government reported 93,979 Mexicans as HIV-positive, out of a population of 106 million. The UN [United Nations] estimates the number infected at 160,000, counting both reported and unreported cases. Although HIV rates among women is rising, men still account for more than 80 percent of the 4,000 new AIDS cases reported every year, says Jorge Saavedra, head of Mexico's national AIDS program.

Dr. Saavedra says it's time to target the core dilemmas facing those most at risk. "How can we start effective prevention campaigns, programs that get information out there about how people can protect themselves, if society rejects those most vulnerable to AIDS? Taking on homophobia is a first step," he says.

Although HIV rates among women is rising, men still account for more than 80 percent of the 4,000 new AIDS cases reported every year.

"We've got to brush aside our puritanical tendencies and talk openly," says Arturo Diaz, spokesman for the anti-homophobia campaign. "If we build tolerance, then perhaps more people will become empowered and get tested. And the more people who know their status, the better our chances of reducing AIDS."

Last month, the government released Mexico's first nationwide survey on discrimination. Although most Mexicans said they disagreed with singling people out because of their sexual preferences, 44 percent of those surveyed said they would not share a house with an HIV-positive person, and 42 percent said they would not seek government intervention if their town banned homosexuals.

Hopefully, says Ricardo Hernandez of Mexico's National Human Rights Commission, the anti-homophobia campaign will improve both doctors' treatment of AIDS patients and the health system's image. In January, the Mexican government's human rights commission reported that nine of every 10 complaints it received from people diagnosed with HIV were directed toward the health sector. Also, activists say businesses still discriminate against homosexuals, though they say concrete numbers are lacking.

In Kyrgyzstan, Homosexuality Is Legal but Opposition Remains

IRIN

IRIN is the humanitarian news and analysis service of the United Nations (UN) Office for the Coordination of Humanitarian Affairs. The opinions expressed do not necessarily reflect those of the United Nations or its member states. In the following viewpoint, IRIN reports on the increase in gay rights in the capital city of Kyrgyzstan but also on the failure of those rights to be recognized both there in the capital and in other parts of the country. Because homosexuality is legal in Kyrgyzstan and punishable by law in neighboring countries, many homosexual people go to Kyrgyzstan from the surrounding countries. However, even in the capital, people who are open about their homosexual orientation are subject to physical, verbal, and psychological abuse. They may be asked to leave bars or restaurants or may lose their jobs. Gay men especially may suffer abuse at the hands of low-ranking police officers. As a result, most gays and lesbians keep their sexual orientation a secret.

As you read, consider the following questions:

1. What is Labrys and its role in the Kyrgyzstan homosexual community?

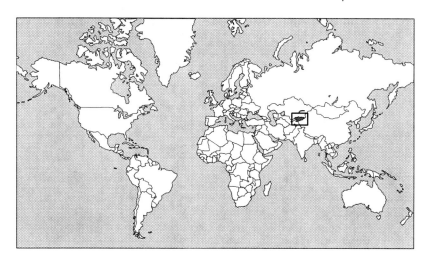

2. About how many people of homosexual orientation does the NGO Oasis estimate live in Bishkek? How many of them keep their sexual orientation a secret?

3. How many men were officially imprisoned or sent to Gulags on charges of sodomy under Soviet rule? When was the Soviet ban on homosexuality lifted?

Bishkek, 11 January 2005 (IRIN)—Kyrgyzstan is known as an island of gay tolerance in an otherwise oppressive region. Some gay people come here from Uzbekistan and Turkmenistan, where homosexuality is punishable by law, in search of a more favourable and accepting environment. The number of gay and lesbian groups in the country is growing as a consequence.

On Saturday a new support group called "Labrys" was launched in the capital, Bishkek, to promote the rights of lesbians. The Labrys, or double-bladed axe, comes from the goddess Demeter (Artemis). It has become a symbol of lesbian and feminist strength and self-sufficiency. "It will organise lesbians, provide them with psychological and legal help, and work on establishing a more tolerant attitude towards lesbians in the country," Anna Dovgopol, leader of the group, funded by money from the Netherlands, told IRIN.

The new organisation will publish a monthly magazine, organise seminars on health issues, and open a telephone hotline and resource centre to offer advice and support. Counselling and cultural events will also be offered. Lesbianism remains very much a taboo in this conservative central Asian nation. "If my family ever finds out that I belong to the group, I will be in deep trouble," one of the women at the launch, who refused to be photographed, told IRIN.

The Reality

Although the attitude to gays and lesbians in Kyrgyzstan is less hostile than in neighbouring states, people of non-traditional sexual orientation, especially gay men, are one of the most oppressed and discriminated groups in the country, according to recent research conducted by Dennis van der Veur for the Dutch HIVOS Fund.

Most gays and lesbians in the country live in the capital, Bishkek, or in the northern part of the country, which is more liberal than other regions. In Bishkek, according to the Oasis NGO [nongovernmental organisation], the only organisation fighting to protect the rights of gay men, there are around 35,000 people of a different sexual orientation. The NGO officially works with just 6,500 of them who are open about their sexual orientation. Others remain undercover.

Those who decide to go public risk physical and verbal abuse, possible loss of work and unwanted attention from the police and authorities.

Veur, who conducted research with more than 50 gay men in the capital, found that they "describe their environment in Kyrgyzstan as negative, hostile and even violent. They refer to the prevalence of discrimination in public places such as bars and restaurants, from where they are often asked to leave."

Around 65 percent of men surveyed said they had been physically or psychologically abused because of their sexual orientation.

"Homosexuals are still poorly informed about their rights," Vladimir Tyupin, the leader of Oasis, said. "Many of them do not know that homosexuality is legal in Kyrgyzstan, and they often are ashamed to ask for legal help. Although senior policemen seem to be understanding, it is the lower ranks, the street patrol officers, who chase and abuse gay men in Kyrgyzstan."

Around 65 percent of men surveyed said they had been physically or psychologically abused because of their sexual orientation.

Theoretically, no one can refuse a gay person a job due to his or her sexual orientation. In reality, homosexuals are sacked under some pretext when their sexuality is revealed, but the official reason for their sacking does not mention their sexual orientation. A recent Oasis opinion poll indicated that most employers in the region would not hire a gay or lesbian if they were aware of the person's sexual orientation.

The situation of homosexuals in prisons is especially daunting as gay men are often openly victimised by inmates and the authorities. Almost half of such people in custody are physically abused, according to research.

Lesbians Also Face Hostility and Rejection

The attitude towards lesbians is less hostile then towards homosexual men. Local tradition allows more freedom for public displays of affection by women. Nevertheless, in Kyrgyzstan lesbians are less visible than gay men and there are no figures for how many there are in the country.

Elena, a gay woman, told IRIN that she had spent most of her life in denial of her sexuality. "At some point I was fed up with hiding, living someone else's life. . . . The most surprising was the reaction from my close friends. Although they are modern [in many of their ways], graduates who have travelled abroad, their reaction to my coming out was shocking. It is a complete rejection."

Despite the fact that the situation in Kyrgyzstan is better than in other central Asian counties, Elena said that she and most of her friends dream about migrating to western Europe or the USA. "We want to feel free to be who we are, to feel like normal people." Lesbian activists say there have been seven known cases so far in which homosexuals from Kyrgyzstan received asylum abroad for "the violation of their human rights" at home.

Dovgopol from Labrys recounted how, in one of the city's cafes, lesbians were refused service due to their sexual orientation and were forced to leave. "They did not complain, because filing a complaint would mean a public and political coming out for lesbians and none of them were willing to do this. They were afraid to be openly lesbian in Kyrgyzstan."

Double Life in the South

In the future, gay rights organisations are planning to expand their activities to other regions such as Osh and Jalalabat in the south of Kyrgyzstan. These are conservative and traditional regions, where most of the population is Muslim. According to Oasis, research among 2,500 gay and lesbians in Osh city suggests that those of a different sexual orientation have no choice but to lead a double life. Many gay men are forced to get married and have children, and hide their sexuality from their family.

There are no support groups protecting the rights of sexual minorities in the south, because it is almost impossible to find someone to lead such an organisation. Many are afraid that participation in such an organisation would ruin their career, and relations with their family and friends.

For lesbians, according to Anna Dovgopol, it is equally difficult: "The society in the provinces is so closed, the topic of homosexuality remains taboo. For a lesbian there it is almost impossible to find other gay people."

"Such tolerance washes out the essence of absolute moral values. Of course, our church will not fight homosexuality with weapons, but we will never tolerate it," Igor Dronov, a senior priest of the church in Bishkek, said.

Condemnation from Religious Leaders

Religious leaders, for the most part, do not exhibit tolerance towards gays and some have even appealed for proactive measures to be taken against them. "I think we should unite our efforts and maybe start punishing people for such behaviour. Thousands of Muslims will be punished by Allah for not preventing, not stopping, lesbians and homosexuals," said the leader of Muslims in Kyrgyzstan, Mufti Lugmar azhi Guahunov.

The Russian Orthodox Church in Kyrgyzstan seems equally hostile to sexual minorities. "Such tolerance washes out the essence of absolute moral values. Of course, our church will not fight homosexuality with weapons, but we will never tolerate it," Igor Dronov, a senior priest of the church in Bishkek, said.

Legal Recognition

During the Soviet period, homosexuality was considered a crime. Article 121 of the USSR [Union of Soviet Socialist Republics] penal code sentenced men for "sodomy" for up to five years in jail. Officially, about 50,000 men were put away in Soviet jails or sent to Gulags [Soviet labor camps] under such charges; the real figure is believed to be much higher.

In Kyrgyzstan the ban on homosexuality was lifted in 1998 after concerted pressure from international human rights organisations. However, the Kyrgyz constitution does not explicitly mention the right to chose one's own sexual orientation.

The Kyrgyz legal system does not appear to be changing to take any further steps to secure the rights of gays and lesbians. It is too early to raise the question of official gay marriages, and legal adoption for same-sex couples in Kyrgyzstan is a long way off, activists say.

Periodical and Internet Sources Bibliography

The following articles have been selected to supplement the diverse views presented in this chapter.

Jim Abrams

"Hate Crimes Bill Approved by Congress, Extends Protection to Gays," *Huffington Post*, October 22, 2009.

GhanaWeb

"Ghana's Laws Do Not Prohibit Homosexuality—Law Lecturer," May 14, 2010. www.ghanaweb.com.

Human Rights Watch

"Iran: Two More Executions for Homosexual Conduct," November 21, 2005. www.hrw.org.

Doug Ireland

"Nigeria: World's Worst Anti-Gay Law May Pass Soon," *Direland* (blog), February 21, 2007. http://direland.typepad.com.

Dominic Kennedy

"Gays Should Be Hanged, Says Iranian Minister," *Times* (London), November 13, 2007.

LifeSiteNews.com

"Homosexual Hate Crime Signed into Law; Chilling Effect on Free Speech, Religion and Importing Materials," April 29, 2004. www.lifesitenews.com.

B.A. Robinson

"Description of U.S. Hate Crime Legislation, from All Viewpoints," ReligiousTolerance.org, June 28, 2009. www.religioustolerance.org.

Robert Tait

"Iran Set to Allow First Transsexual Marriage," *Guardian*, September 11, 2009.

Pete Vere

"Catholicism—A Hate Crime in Canada?" *Catholic Exchange*, June 4, 2008.

Alison Walkley

"Gay Men Become Trans Women in Iran," Suite101.com, February 26, 2008. http://transgenderism.suite101.com.

GLOBALVIEWPOINTS

CHAPTER 4

Homosexuality
and Family

In Australia, Same-Sex Couples Should Have the Right to Marry

Jennifer Power

Jennifer Power won the CASS PhD publishing prize for her thesis Movement, Knowledge, Emotion: Gay Activists and the Australian AIDS Movement, *completed in 2007 at the Australian National University. In the following viewpoint, Power argues for the legalization of gay marriage. Although marriage is a vehicle of oppression for women and gay couples, she contends, it is something that is allowed for heterosexuals but not for homosexuals, which denies them full citizenship. Therefore, homosexuals should be allowed to marry, so that the definition of marriage and the social contract it embodies can be further defined to suit today's society.*

As you read, consider the following questions:

1. What is the feminist and Marxist critique of the institution of marriage, according to Power?
2. According to the author, why are marriage laws a clear target for gay and lesbian activism?
3. At this point in history, what two things does the campaign for gay marriage do, according to the author?

Jennifer Power, "Something Old, Something New," *Arena Magazine*, vol. 83, June–July 2006, p 22. Copyright © 2006 Arena Printing and Publications Pty. Ltd. Reprinted with permission.

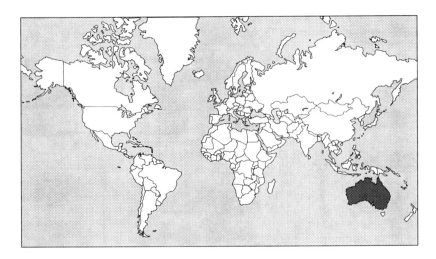

A friend of mine recently recounted a story about some friends of hers, a lesbian couple, who had had a falling out with some friends of theirs, a gay male couple. The two couples had fought because the men were planning to marry. If the ACT [Australian Capital Territory] Government was successful in passing [its] bill allowing civil unions between same-sex couples, the two men were planning a weekend trip to Canberra. Their lesbian friends were horrified; they couldn't understand why two gay men would willingly submit themselves to the traditionally heterosexual and patriarchal institution that is marriage.

My first reaction to this story was: 'Is this really something to lose friends over?' Surely marriage is simply about individual choice. If these two men want to be married then their friends should be supportive. Isn't the issue of allowing gay marriage simply one about freedom of choice and equality?

But of course it is not that simple. The fact that there is such vocal critique of gay marriage within the gay community itself is indicative of the fact that the issue isn't just a case of 'for or against'.

The political struggle around gay marriage has led to a polarisation of the debate. It is framed as a choice between competing agendas: conservative versus progressive. Progressives argue along the lines of human rights and equity: The regulations around marriage should be adapted to ensure all people have the right to marry their chosen partner. The conservative argument is that the institution of heterosexual marriage is sacrosanct and cannot be altered. 'Marriage' is a universally understood union between a man and a woman, not something that evolves to suit the times.

But what about the problem of marriage itself?

Decades of feminist and Marxist critique of the institution of marriage seem absent in a debate framed by a 'for or against' dichotomy. Where is the scope for a critique of marriage as a social and economic institution? Many conservatives argue that marriage must be protected at all costs because it is the fundamental institution of our society. They're right; marriage is the fundamental institution of capitalism. From its inception it has been a social contract rooted in private property laws. Marriage regenerates and maintains the workforce free of charge and history has shown that, as an institution, marriage contributes to the oppression of women. Couples may challenge gender norms and the sexual division of labour within their own home, but at a structural level the institution of marriage remains steadfastly committed to patriarchal and heterosexual norms.

The political struggle around gay marriage has led to a polarisation of the debate. It is framed as a choice between competing agendas: conservative versus progressive.

It's not surprising that when it comes to marriage many gay people are asking: 'Why do we want in?' In fact, marriage is increasingly not the relationship of choice for many heterosexual couples. It almost seems strange that in a climate where marriage is decreasing in popularity, conservatives aren't supporting a group that is actively promoting the social benefits of marriage.

While same-sex marriage creates new boundaries around the genders of those involved in the contract, it doesn't necessarily open new conceptual space for imagining relationships and family. The fundamental model of marriage still stands, and many would argue that the capitalist state doesn't care about the gender of a married couple so long as the institution is doing its job.

Does same-sex marriage really create greater acceptance for people whose sexualities defy the norm? Or does it further entrench a traditional, nuclear family model? A model that doesn't relate very closely to the lives of thousands of gay people.

Ultimately, would legalisation of gay marriage represent radical social change? No one involved in gay politics is kidding themselves. No one believes that legalisation of gay marriage signals the end of oppression. But currently, gay couples are denied the right to engage in a common social contract to which heterosexual couples have access. Marriage laws are a clear target for gay and lesbian activism because they represent an achievable change. It is a barrier to equality that can be overcome within the existing social framework. And, without doubt, there are many gay couples that, on a personal level, don't have political axes to grind with the concept of marriage; they simply want to walk down the aisle.

Marriage is still a significant social ritual, and the right to engage in marriage is a staple of Western citizenship. Without marriage rights, gay relationships have no rituals of acknowledgement and gay people are symbolically denied full citizenship. This creates an interesting tension in the conservative agenda that explains why you see people like conservative Queensland Liberal MP [member of Parliament] Warren Entsch actively campaigning for gay marriage. Disallowing gay

Gay and Lesbian Eligibility for Adoption and Foster Care by Australian Province or Territory, 2009

	Eligible to Apply for Adoption?	Eligible to Apply to Become Foster Carers?
New South Wales	Same-sex couples—no Individual gays and lesbians—yes	yes
Victoria	Same-sex couples—no Individual gays and lesbians—yes	yes
Queensland	Same-sex couples—no Individual gays and lesbians—yes	yes
Western Australia	Same-sex couples—yes Individual gays and lesbians—yes	yes
South Australia	Same-sex couples—no Individual gays and lesbians—yes	yes
Tasmania	Same-sex couples—partially Individual gays and lesbians—yes	yes
Northern Territory	Same-sex couples—no Individual gays and lesbians—yes	yes

TAKEN FROM: Gay & Lesbian Rights Lobby, "Inquiry into Adoption by Same-Sex Couples: Submission of the Gay & Lesbian Rights Lobby (NSW)," January 2009, pp. 25–26. http://glrl.org.au.

marriage contravenes basic liberal notions of a level playing field. Full citizenship for nationals, freedom and individual choice are theoretically at the heart of Western liberalism.

But marriage clearly isn't a totally 'free' arrangement. Marriage cannot be defined by individuals outside the boundaries of some form of social agreement. Marriage is a social contract that, by definition, must have agreed-upon boundaries for it to be meaningful. If marriage could be on any terms between anyone—or anything—it wouldn't be a contract of social significance. Howard has been at pains to point this out. What we recognise as marriage, he argues, must be defined by community standards, not by individuals. In Howard's view, the Australian public would not accept gay marriage because Australians understand marriage to be a union between a man and woman (how he knows exactly what the public feels is not entirely clear). As far as Howard is concerned, the fact that gay people want to be married is not an argument for considering gay marriage; marriage is, and will always be, heterosexual.

Perhaps, then, what is radical about campaigning for gay marriage is that it demonstrates that social institutions aren't static entities.

It is this logic that allows Howard and his cronies to maintain that banning gay marriage does not constitute discrimination against gay men and women. He presents the current heterosexual boundaries of the marriage contract as ahistorical and universal—not open to change.

But marriage is not something that has universally accepted and unchanging codes. Even within our own culture the idea of arranged marriage was once a social norm, something that even Howard would probably consider undesirable in the current social climate. Perhaps, then, what is radical about campaigning for gay marriage is that it demonstrates that social institutions aren't static entities; they are products of society and as society changes so to[o] do institutions such as marriage. There is nothing natural about marriage. It is a socially derived formality and society determines the codes that define it.

Fighting for gay marriage could be seen as cow-tailing to an institution that has long been a source of social oppression for women and gay couples. But perhaps while gay men and lesbians are denied access to such an institution they are also denied the legitimacy to challenge the basis of marriage. Maybe full rights of citizenship are needed to gain the confidence and authority to take the next step?

The gay marriage debate exposes the conservative social agenda of the current government. Howard has claimed that he is simply following public opinion on issues like gay marriage: his legislation dutifully follows the will of his constituents. Of course, when it comes to industrial relations regulations or economic reform he prides himself on his capacity for leadership and reform—he is showing the Australian public where they need to go.

In the end, context is everything. What is conservative in some instances is radical in others. At this point in history, the campaign for gay marriage does challenge a conservative social agenda and it does subvert the idea that marriage is innately about heterosexual unions. In this context, that's got to be a good thing.

South Africa Should Not Legalize Adoption for Same-Sex Couples

Africa Christian Action

Africa Christian Action (ACA) is an organization that works for Christian reform in South Africa by conducting research, disseminating information, and engaging in activism. In the following viewpoint, ACA argues that children of homosexuals are unsociable, do poorly in school, and are more likely to become homosexuals themselves. In addition, the organization says, homosexuals are prone to substance abuse, crime, and violence; they have shorter life expectancies and their relationships are less committed. For all these reasons, and because the Bible opposes homosexuality, the ACA concludes that South Africa should not allow homosexual couples to adopt.

As you read, consider the following questions:

1. What statistics does the viewpoint provide about the consequences of single-parent and fatherless homes in the United States?

2. According to the viewpoint, an article published in the *Journal of Interpersonal Violence* found that what percentage of lesbians surveyed reported incidents of interpersonal violence or physical abuse?

Africa Christian Action, "Family: What About the Children? (homosexual adoption)," Africa Christian Action, 2003. Reproduced by permission.

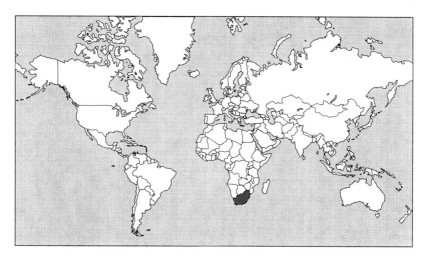

3. What does the viewpoint say is the life expectancy of homosexual men as opposed to the life expectancy of heterosexual men?

Should people involved in homosexual or lesbian relationships be allowed to adopt children?

The High Court [of South Africa] is presently [2003] considering whether homosexual and lesbian couples should be allowed to co-adopt children. Are children who grow up in single-sex parented homes advantaged or disadvantaged?

Tragic Consequences

These statistics show the tragic consequences of fatherless and single-parent homes in the United States:

- 63% of youth suicides are from fatherless homes.

- 85% of all children that exhibit behavioural disorders come from fatherless homes.

- 80% of rapists motivated with displaced anger come from fatherless homes.

- 71% of all high school dropouts come from fatherless homes.

- 75% of all adolescent patients in drug abuse centres come from fatherless homes.

- 85% of all youths sitting in prisons grew up in a fatherless home.

While this applies to children who grow up in fatherless homes, mothers are equally important in the lives of children and the results of "motherless" homes are equally tragic. Children who grow up with two mothers and no father, and those who grow up with two fathers and no mother, will be horribly handicapped in life.

Dr Sotirios Sarantakos from Charles Sturt University, Australia, did research comparing primary school children in married, cohabiting heterosexual and homosexual couples. Children in normal marriages faired the best, and children in homosexual homes the worst. Children of homosexual couples scored the lowest in language ability, mathematics and sport. They were more timid, reserved, unwilling to work in a team or talk about home lives and holidays. They felt "uncomfortable when having to work with students of a sex different from the parent they lived with" and were the least sociable. Although homosexual couples gave their children "more freedom", married couples cared for and directed their children most. Children of married parents had clear future plans, while the children of homosexuals and cohabiters wanted to leave school and get a job as soon as possible. Children of homosexuals were "more confused about their gender" and more effeminate (irrespective of their gender).

It is not fair of our society, our government and our courts to establish public policy that encourages this social engineering and pretends that homosexual "families" are normal, healthy and desirable. Instead, public policy should work toward mitigating the harmful effects of divorce and single parenting that result in motherless and fatherless homes—not promoting it!

Former lesbian Cherie Tayler had three children by artificial insemination. Her lesbian partner shared the parenting. After the breakup of their 16-year relationship, Cherie admitted that her life as a lesbian has been spurred on by her unloving mother and sexually abusive father. She said that having children had been a cruel mistake. She reported on a *60 Minutes* TV documentary that she saw the hurt in her children's faces every day. Her 11-year-old son wanted to know about his father's job, what he looked like, the colour of his eyes—and Cherie was unable to answer. She said, "I (now) believe that children should have the best opportunities in life. The best way they can have a balanced view of what is normal is with heterosexual parents."

Children who grow up with two mothers and no father, and those who grow up with two fathers and no mother, will be horribly handicapped in life.

It does not matter whether we think homosexuality (the act of "mating" with a member of the same sex) is normal or deviant, emotionally healthy or not, the fact is that we should do what is best for the children. People who live homosexual lives say that they have a right to do what they want in their bedrooms and private lives. But adopting children is not about their "private" lives as it intrudes into the lives of children who will not have a choice, and are not old enough to make a mature and informed choice. Special privileges, like adoption, for men or women who engage in homosexuality, are hotly debated worldwide, with the vast majority of countries, and the vast majority of people across the world, saying "No, let's stick to what is best for the children."

Social Experiments Are Harmful to Children

A study by two pro-homosexual sociologists from the University of Southern California, Judith Stacey and Timothy Biblarz, showed that these children "seem to grow up to be more open to homoerotic relations (getting involved in homosexuality)." Stacey said that in the past "sympathetic researchers" have defensively stressed an absence of difference, but a reevaluation of past studies showed that there are significant differences. Homosexual activists were pleased about this. Aimee Gelnaw, director of Family Pride Coalition (a prohomosexual organisation) responded to the research, "Of course our kids are going to be different. They are growing up in a different social context." Kate Kendall, head of the San Francisco-based National Center for Lesbian Rights said homosexuals should be elated by the study which shows that "our kids are somewhat more likely to identify as lesbian and gay."

But is this best for children? British MP [member of Parliament] Julian Brazier says, "This sort of social experiment may be exciting for the people who take part in it but they should ask themselves whether it is in the best interests of the child."

Even in those homosexual relationships, which the partners consider "committed," the meaning of "committed" typically means something radically different from marriage.

Cornelia Oddie of the U.K. [United Kingdom]-based Family and Youth Concern think tank says, "It must be extra confusing for the children. With homosexual couples the majority of their friends would be presumably part of the homosexual culture, so the children grow up with a skewed idea of relationships. This is bound to give children an unbalanced view of social and sexual relationships."

The implications are severe. With the acceptance of two homosexuals as joint parents, the family is torn from its traditional and God-inspired balance of a mother and a father

Opinions of Nontraditional Adoption in the United Kingdom

Type of Family	Percentage of Public Who Does Not Think Family Should Be Allowed to Adopt Children
Single Woman	30%
Single Man	43%
Gay Male Couple	40%
Gay Female Couple	36%

TAKEN FROM: BBC News, "Concern over Gay Adoption Views," November 12, 2008. http://news.bbc.co.uk. http://news.bbc.co.uk/2/hi/7722745.stm.

both giving of their commitment, love and essence to the children. What kinds of homes can homosexuals and lesbians offer children?

Even in those homosexual relationships, which the partners consider "committed," the meaning of "committed" typically means something radically different from marriage.

In the Triangle Project study of homosexual men in Cape Town [South Africa], 47% of respondents said that they were currently in a relationship, yet only 13.3% of respondents had had only one partner in the past year. 60% of the men who were currently "in a relationship" admitted to having had "sex" with people other than their partners in the past year.

In the book, *The Male Couple: How Relationships Develop*, the authors, two homosexual lecturers, report a study of 156 men in homosexual relationships lasting from one to 37 years. Only seven couples had a totally exclusive sexual relationship and of these, the men had all been together for less than five years. In other words, all the so-called "couples" with a relationship lasting more than five years had incorporated some outside sexual activity into their relationships.

While homosexuals, particularly lesbians, propagate the idea of the lesbian or homosexual home as one of peace and equality, the truth is that homosexual relationships are far more violent than heterosexual marriages. The U.S. Department of Justice's Bureau of Justice Statistics reports that married women in normal families experience the lowest rate of violence compared with women in other types of relationships. Consider these studies of homosexual relationships:

- *The Journal of Interpersonal Violence* published an article entitled "Letting Out the Secret: Violence in Lesbian Relationships." Researchers found that 90% of the lesbians surveyed had been recipients of one or more acts of verbal aggression from their intimate partners during the year prior to this study. 31% of women in lesbian relationships reported one or more incidents of physical abuse.

- A survey of 1,099 lesbians found that "slightly more than half of the [lesbians] reported that they had been abused by a female lover/partner. The most frequent forms of abuse were verbal/emotional/psychological abuse and combined physical-psychological abuse."

- In their book *Men Who Beat the Men Who Love Them: Battered Gay Men and Domestic Violence*, D. Island and P. Letellier report that "the incidence of domestic violence among gay men is nearly double that in the heterosexual population."

Crime and Substance Abuse

A study of 4340 adults in five metropolitan areas of the USA showed that bisexuals and homosexuals (about 4% of the sample) compared to heterosexuals:

- exposed themselves sexually to more different bodies (more frequently admitting to participating in orgies and reported larger numbers of sexual partners);

- more frequently participated in socially disruptive sex (e.g., deliberate infection of others, cheating in marriage, making obscene phone calls);

- more frequently reported engaging in socially disruptive activities (e.g., criminality, shoplifting, tax cheating); and

- more frequently exposed themselves to biological hazards (e.g., fisting, bestiality, ingestion of faeces and sadomasochism).

- A study published in *Nursing Research* found that lesbians are three times more likely to abuse alcohol and suffer from other compulsive behaviours than heterosexual women. The study found that: Like most problem drinkers, 91% of the participants had abused other drugs as well as alcohol, and many reported compulsive difficulties with food (34%), co-dependency on people (29%), sex (11%), and money (6%)." In addition, "46% had been heavy drinkers with frequent drunkenness."

- The Triangle Project survey of homosexual men in Cape Town in 2000 found that 68% of men had used at least one recreational drug in the past year. 41% had used marijuana, 40% used ecstacy, 36% used poppers and 25% used cocaine. Acid and speed were used by about a fifth of the men.

- A study in *[International] Family Planning Perspectives* showed that male homosexuals were at greatly increased risk for alcoholism: "Among men, by far the most important risk group consisted of homosexual and bisexual men, who were more than nine times as likely as heterosexual men to have a history of problem drinking."

- The *Washington Blade*, a homosexual newspaper, reports that "various studies on lesbian health suggest

that certain cancer risk factors occur with greater frequency in this population. These factors include higher
rates of smoking, alcohol use, poor diet and being
overweight."

Note also that homosexuals have shorter life spans than
other people. A study in the United States found that the median age of death of married men was 75 and unmarried heterosexual men, 71. By comparison, homosexual men who died
of non-AIDS causes, had a median age of death of 42 (41
years for those men who had a long-term sexual partner and
43 for those who did not). Homosexuals who had long-term
partners lived shorter than those who do not. The study also
found that homosexuals were 24 times more likely to commit
suicide and had a traffic-accident death rate 18 times the rate
of comparably aged white males. The 140 lesbians surveyed
had a median age of death of 45 and exhibited high rates of
violent death and cancer as compared to women in general.
The study showed that 20% of lesbians died of murder, suicide or accident—a rate 512 times higher than that of white
females of similar age.

---

*Children in homosexual homes score lower grades and
are more sexually confused and unsociable than other
children.*

Against God and Harmful to Children

God's Word is clear that only a man and a woman can enter
into marriage, and this is the foundation for the family. Gen-
esis 2:24 reads, "Therefore a man shall leave his father and
mother and be joined to his wife, and they shall become one
flesh." Malachi 2:15 says that God made a man and his wife
one because "he seeks godly offspring." For those who stray
from the wisdom of God, the results are tragic. These statistics
show that homosexual homes are less stable, more unfaithful

and relationships are shorter, and there is more drug and alcohol abuse and domestic violence. Children in homosexual homes score lower grades and are more sexually confused and unsociable than other children. If one homosexual couple wins the right to co-adopt children, the door will [be] opened for this social experiment, without further research, study or discussion into the issue.

In Canada, Legalizing Same-Sex Marriage Has Worked Well

Mercedes Allen

Mercedes Allen is a Canadian writer, a transgender activist, and the founder of AlbertaTrans.org. In the following viewpoint, she points out that Canada has had same-sex marriage for a number of years. In that time, she says, same-sex marriage has not weakened the institution of marriage, nor increased polygamy, nor resulted in persecution of religious institutions. In general, she concludes that none of the dire consequences predicted by opponents of same-sex marriage have come to pass in Canada. Therefore, she says, the claims that same-sex marriage will have disastrous results in America and other places are unfounded.

As you read, consider the following questions:

1. According to Allen, how have divorce statistics in Canada changed between 2004, just before same-sex marriage was legalized, and 2007?
2. What polygamous group does Allen discuss, and why is the government having difficulty prosecuting them?
3. What happened to Canada's birth rate between 2004–2005 and 2007–2008, according to Allen?

Mercedes Allen, "Same-Sex Marriage: Three Years On," Bilerico Project, October 14, 2008. Reproduced by permission.

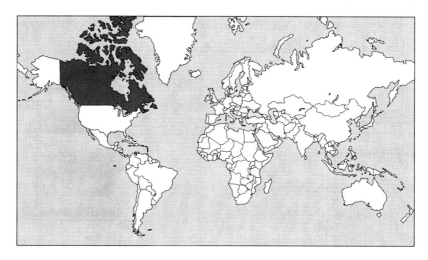

If people in California, Arizona, Florida, and anywhere else that same-sex marriage is being debated find this [viewpoint] useful, they are welcome to distribute it. I'm writing this because a lot of people in America are forgetting that there is already an over 3-year-long test case slightly north of them, in a nation with a culture that closely mirrors American culture at times, and which can help sort the facts from the fearmongering: Canada.

Canada Has Already Legalized Same-Sex Marriage

Same-sex marriage has been legal in Canada since July 19th, 2005, following a chain of events that began in a Court of Appeal in Ontario in 2003. It was the third country in the world to legalize it, after the Netherlands (2000) and Belgium (2003), and happened in a few provinces before being recognized nationwide. In the end, the issue still came to a vote in the House of Commons (instead of, as many in the religious right will tell you, legislating done by judges) and it passed with 158 MPs [members of Parliament] for it (versus 133 against). When the Conservatives came to power, they attempted to reopen the debate, and this motion was defeated by a vote of

175 to 123 on December 7th, 2006. By that time, people were used to over a full year of same-sex marriage existing, and typically called it a "non-issue." And somehow, the country failed to implode. Where hard statistics are available (they're amazingly hard to find), I present them below; at times, common sense also needs to be remembered.

Claim: "Same-sex marriage will weaken the institution of marriage."

Okay, that's a pretty broad statement. First, we need to define things. If we're referring to statistical rates of marriages, they have continued to climb along with the population. If we're talking about divorces, there has been no quantifiable change.

In Canada, divorces hovered at just under 38% from 2000 to 2002, the year before the provinces of Ontario and British Columbia, along with the Yukon territory, legalized same-sex marriage in their jurisdiction. In 2004 (just before the legalization across the country) it rose to 41.3%. Since then, it has dropped again, slightly. For 2007, I have an unconfirmed number of 37%.

Divorces among same-sex couples specifically have been significantly small thus far—marriage was first available to some provinces in June of 2003, but two years later only two same-sex divorces were recorded, compared to thousands of marriages having taken place in that same time frame. Perhaps same-sex marriages are hard-won enough and serious enough decisions that people do not enter into them as frivolously as opposite-sex couples.

From ReligiousTolerance.org:

Among many religious and social liberals, giving same-sex couples the same marriage rights (and rites) as opposite-sex couples has already had one positive effect on marriage in Canada: It has brought many same-sex couples who are enthusiastic supporters of marriage into the institution. Marriage in North America has been suffering lately, as increasing numbers of couples decide to simply live together rather than marry. Also, large numbers of married couples are separating and/or divorcing.

Divorces among same-sex couples have been significantly small thus far.

So while opposite-sex couples have not been noticeably impacted by same-sex marriage legislation, the institution of marriage has achieved a kind of renaissance in Canada—albeit one that homophobes simply don't want to acknowledge. In comparison, Barna Research Group discovered in 1999 that divorce rates among faith populations were considerably higher for conservative Christians, and so far no one has been able to attribute that to the advent of same-sex marriage.

I don't have any comparative rates of infidelity between heterosexual and gay couples (reliable studies, i.e., with no likely bias either way, appear not to exist at this point in time).

Also keep in mind that marriage was not always the institution that we understand it to be today. Prior to the Roman Catholic Church's assertion of authority over legal partnerships at the Council of Trent [a 16th-century council that established many Catholic doctrines] (1545–1563), it was far less formal, and for hundreds of years following that event, it was still largely reserved for the wealthy, often used to strategically unite families for monetary and political gain. For commoners, the "common law" had to suffice. The effect of same-sex marriage pales compared to the effect of Catholicization and economic changes over the centuries—not to mention the advent of divorce itself. Similar claims of "destroying marriage" had been made about interracial marriages prior to 1958, and negative effects from that have also not materialized (unless you're a white supremacist who believes in racial purity).

New Zealand Should Allow Same-Sex Adoption

We [New Zealand] would not be the first country to allow same-sex adoption. Countries with whom we share cultural, historical and legal bonds have already taken that step. England and Wales have allowed same-sex adoption since 2002. Scotland has just recently [2009] passed legislation allowing same-sex adoption. Western Australia and the ACT [Australian Capital Territory] are among states in our nearest neighbor which allow same-sex couples to adopt. The list goes on: New York, California, Michigan, Quebec, British Columbia, Ontario and the Northwest Territories as well as several countries in Europe.

Recently, the European Court of Human Rights, in a case referred to it from France, allowed a lesbian couple to adopt a child.

Quite apart from the fact that the current prohibition runs counter to the NZBORA [New Zealand Bill of Rights Act 1990] and the HRA [Human Rights Act 1993], we are lagging behind many other countries.

Paul von Dadelszen,
"A New Adoption Act for the New Millenium,"
Family Court of New Zealand Web site,
August 17, 2009. www.justice.govt.nz.

Little Evidence of Harm to Children

Claim: "Same-sex marriage will pave the way for polygamists, incest and all sorts of other immoral couplings."

In fact, Canada does have an issue with polygamy, centering around a Mormon community in Bountiful, B.C. [British Columbia]. This year [2008], authorities were reluctant to move on claims of abuses in that community, because they felt it likely that they would lose a court challenge . . . not be-cause of same-sex marriage, but because of the Mormons' freedom of religion.

And incest, which is illegal in the eyes of the Criminal Code of Canada, certainly has not had any sort of surge in popularity or acceptance since the legalization of SSM [same-sex marriage].

Claim: "Two mommies or two daddies cannot adequately parent."

Although it has been suppressed by the current Conserva-tive government in Canada, an extensive report drawn up for the Department of Justice took a thorough look at families in which children are raised by same-sex parents. The report found:

> The strongest conclusion that can be drawn from the em-pirical literature is that the vast majority of studies show that children living with two mothers and children living with a mother and father have the same levels of social competence. A few studies suggest that children with two lesbian mothers may have marginally better social compe-tence than children in traditional nuclear families. . . .

The conservative right often advances this belief along with certain assumptions about male and female roles in parenting. It is believed by many of these groups that men were meant to lead, make decisions and support families fi-nancially, while women were meant solely to parent (i.e., ca-reers for women negatively impact the family) and to submit to their husbands. Dysfunction can be found among as many conservative and religious households as any other house-holds, while considerable functionality can be found among families where gay males or lesbian couples are parenting. It helps when at least one parent is able to focus on the child's upbringing and well-being, and foster communication. The conservative stance on this point reveals a particular misogyny at work.

Liberal studies sometimes find that children of same-sex couples tend to develop less bigoted attitudes; even if dismissed as biased studies, they still tend to pass muster as anecdotal evidence.

Children who have been raised by GLBTQ couples simply usually become more comfortable with accepting their own innate orientation, whether straight, gay or bi.

Claim: "Raising a child in a same-sex household will expose [him or her] to homophobia."

There are no existing quantifiable statistics on this, so while possibly true, the same argument still holds little water when applied to interracial marriages, where children of a mixed-race couple might be subject to racial discrimination. In the latter example, modern society recognizes that it is the bigotry that is of concern—not the race, faith, gender, age, etc., that it targets.

Claim: "Children raised by gays or lesbians will become homosexuals themselves."

Again, there is no concrete statistical analysis of this at present. Mental health professionals, sexuality researchers and anecdotal evidence tend to concur that children who have been raised by GLBTQ [gay, lesbian, bisexual, transgender, and queer] couples simply usually become more comfortable with accepting their own innate orientation, whether straight, gay or bi [bisexual]. Even this is not always 100%. As a trans [transgender] advocate, I am familiar with at least one instance where a trans youth was kicked out of a same-sex household (one parent of which was a biological parent) in part because of transphobic bias, so reality is far more complex than assumptions and conjecture would like to admit.

More than that, though, is that despite fundamentalists' contention that being gay is a choice, the science and anecdotal evidence still indicate otherwise.

This argument also assumes that being gay in itself is something that is unacceptable and undesirable, but I suppose that's obvious.

No Special Rights

Claim: *"Allowing same-sex marriage gives special rights to gay couples."*

No, it gives equal rights, to GLBTQ couples. How difficult is this to get? Three years on, gay couples are not considered preferential in Canada, nor are they more protected than heterosexual couples, legally, socially or otherwise.

Claim: *"Allowing same-sex marriage is another major step toward religious persecution."*

Three years on, gay couples are not considered preferential in Canada, nor are they more protected than heterosexual couples, legally, socially or otherwise.

Religious institutions are given an exemption from having to perform same-sex marriages and also have significant freedom from anti-bigotry/anti-discrimination actions through the Charter of Rights and Freedoms. Canada's hate speech laws also provide an exemption based on religious beliefs, limited only by calls to action. A recent Human Rights Commission ruling against Rev. Stephen Boissoin hinged largely on the fact that in his letter to the *Red Deer Advocate*, Boissoin suggested that "something should be done" about homosexuals (my paraphrasing—the actual text of the letter has been sealed and is unavailable due to the court case and its ruling). And, of course, just over a week after the letter to the editor was published "something" was done, in the case of a teen being beaten for being perceived as gay—an action that judges linked circumstantially to the letter.

Religious institutions in Canada have not stopped preaching against homosexuality, have rarely been taken to task for their words, and freedom of religion is still being weighed heavily in instances where the question comes up. . . .

Claim: "Allowing same-sex marriage will erode the Christian faith."

Possibly true, but not dramatically and probably not single-handedly. The number of Canadians who believe in God declined slightly, to 72%.

Claim: "Allowing same-sex marriage will help facilitate a general acceptance of homosexuality."

Yes, it does. This only matters to those who think that tolerance is a particularly bad thing.

Claim: "Recognizing same-sex marriage will cost too much in spousal benefits."

Marriage injects a considerable amount of money into the economy and costs no more than it would have if the beneficiary coincidentally happened to be a married heterosexual. Businesses in Canada have not suffered significantly due to the introduction of same-sex marriage—certainly, it is never raised as an issue here. This argument is as discriminatory as it would be if the costs of benefits for interracial marriages, marriages involving people of certain ages or marriages of low-income couples were called into question.

Many Reasons for, and Forms of, Marriage

Claim: "Procreation is the heart of marriage, and is not possible among same-sex couples."

Overlooking the fact that artificial insemination makes procreation possible between same-sex couples, or that many adults are infertile and would be exempted from marriage eligibility by the same logic, the earth's population does not appear to be diminishing any time soon. Canada's birth rate rose from 339,270 in 2004/5 to 364,085 in 2007/8, so people can breathe a little easier. We didn't stop being fruitful and multiplying.

This argument assumes that child rearing is the sole focus of marriage, overlooking the human needs for companionship, mutual commitment and support and other crucial aspects present in marriage.

Claim: "9/11 [September 11, 2001, terrorist attacks on the United States], Hurricane Katrina, etc., are God's punishment for the nation's tolerance of homosexuality."

I'm guessing most rational people can see through that one. And while it's not right to assume that we'd never be the target of terrorism or be struck by a major national disaster, I suspect that the relative lack of such things in Canada tends to rule out causation.

Claim: "Marriage has always been between one man and one woman."

Okay, there's no relevant statistical info from Canada that addresses this one, but same-sex unions had been recognized at various times through history, including ancient Egypt, Native cultures with two-spirit traditions [that is, traditions of mixed-gender individuals], classical Greece, republican and imperial Rome, pre-Christian ("pagan") Europe, and various African tribes. It also persists among some "untouched" remote cultures, such as in Samoa, along with trans-related traditions. Hebrew scriptures describe different family traditions that weren't always the one man + one woman ethic of today, including polygamous relationships involving concubinage (i.e., the "father" of both Judaic and Arabic cultures, Abraham—he had a first-born child by a concubine and then a child with his preferred wife, and their descendants have been fighting ever since).

Claim: "It's icky."

Get over it.

Legalizing Same-Sex Marriage in Canada Was a Mistake

Michael Coren

Michael Coren is a Canadian author, columnist, and television personality who hosts The Michael Coren Show. *In the following viewpoint, he argues that same-sex marriage weakens the institution of marriage. He states that allowing same-sex marriage may make it difficult to outlaw polygamy. Further, he says same-sex marriage separates love from the creation of children and that it will hurt children who are brought up without a male or female role model. He argues that, as a result, same-sex marriage will eventually hurt Canadian society.*

As you read, consider the following questions:

1. With whom does Coren say the deconstruction of marriage began?
2. What does Coren say is the most significant interest of the state in marriage?
3. How long does Coren believe it will take to appreciate the full consequences of allowing same-sex marriage?

What makes the national mistake of legalizing same-sex marriage unique in Canadian history is that to even discuss the issue is considered by many, particularly our elites,

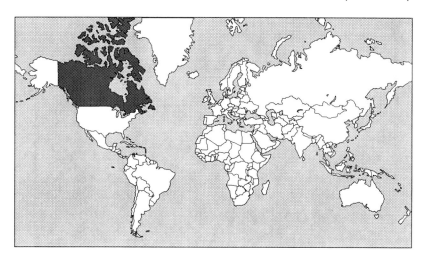

to be at the very least in extraordinarily bad taste. Although this is a valid and vital debate about social policy, anyone critiquing the status quo is likely to be marginalized as hateful, extreme or simply mad. Social conservatives aren't just wrong, they're evil.

Number, Gender, Age, and Blood

The discussion, we are told, is over. Which is what triumphalist bullies have said for centuries after they win a battle. In this case, the intention is to marginalize anyone who dares to still speak out. In other words, to silence them.

It's important to emphasize that this is not really about homosexuality at all, and has nothing to do with homosexual people living together. Opponents of same-sex marriage may have ethical and religious objections to homosexuality, but they are irrelevant to the central argument. Which is not about the rights of a sexual minority but the status and meaning of marriage.

Indeed, the deconstruction of marriage began not with the gay community asking for the right to marry but with the heterosexual world rejecting it. The term "common law marriage" said it all. Marriage is many things, but it is never com-

Gay Marriage Will Undo Civilization

The irrelevance of marriage to gay people will create a series of perfectly reasonable, perfectly unanswerable questions: If gays can aim at marriage, yet do without it equally well, who are we to demand it of one another? Who are women to demand it of men? Who are parents to demand it of their children's lovers—or to prohibit their children from taking lovers until parents decide arbitrarily they are "mature" or "ready"? By what right can government demand that citizens obey arbitrary and culturally specific kinship rules—rules about incest and the age of consent, rules that limit marriage to twosomes? . . . The whole set of fundamental, irrational assumptions that make marriage such a burden and such a civilizing force can easily be undone.

Sam Schulman,
"The Worst Thing About Gay Marriage,"
Weekly Standard, *June 1, 2009.*
www.weeklystandard.com.

mon. Yet with this semantic and legal revolution, desire and convenience replaced commitment and dedication. The qualifications, so to speak, were lowered.

The four great and historic qualifications for marriage always have been number, gender, age and blood.

And one does indeed have to qualify for marriage; just as one has, for example, to qualify for a pension or a military medal. People who have not reached the age of retirement don't qualify for a pension, people who don't serve in the armed forces don't qualify for a military medal. It's not a question of equality but requirement. A human right is intrinsic, a social institution is not.

The four great and historic qualifications for marriage always have been number, gender, age and blood. Two people, male and female, over a certain age and not closely related. Mainstream and responsible societies have sometimes changed the age of maturity, but incest has always been condemned and, by its nature, died out because of retardation.

As for polygamy, it's making something of a comeback—and here begin the objections.

For the first time not only in Canadian but in world history we are purposefully creating and legitimizing families where there will be either no male or no female role model and parent.

A Slippery Slope

Whenever this is mentioned by critics of same-sex marriage we are accused of using the slippery-slope argument. Sorry, some slopes are slippery. Polygamy is an ancient tradition within Islam—and was in Sephardic Judaism and some Asian cultures. When the precedent of gay marriage is combined with the freedom of religion defence, the courts will have a difficult time rejecting it.

At the moment, the Muslim community is not sufficiently politically comfortable to pursue the issue; and the clearly deranged polygamous sects on the aesthetic as well as geographical fringes of Canadian society cloud any reasonable debate. But the argument will certainly come and the result is largely inevitable. If love is the only criterion for marriage who are we to judge the love between a man and his wives?

The state, though, should have a duty to judge and to do so based on its own interests. The most significant of which is its continued existence, meaning that we have to produce children. As procreation is the likely, if not essential, result of marriage between a man and a woman, it is in the interests of the state to encourage marriage.

Of course lesbian couples can have an obliging friend assist them in having a baby, and gay men can adopt or have an obliging friend have one for them, but this is hardly the norm and hardly going to guarantee the longevity of a stable society. Just as significant, it smashes the fundamental concept of a child being produced through an act of love. The donation of bodily fluid by an anonymous person, or that obliging friend again, is an act not of love but of lust, indifference, profit or a mere, well, helping hand.

For the first time not only in Canadian but in world history we are purposefully creating and legitimizing families where there will be either no male or no female role model and parent. Anyone who speaks of uncles, aunts, communities and villages raising children has no real understanding of family life. Single-parent families exist and are sometimes excellent and, obviously, not every mother/father family is a success. But to consciously create unbalanced families where children can never enjoy the profound difference between man and woman, mother and father, is dangerous social engineering.

We made a terrible mistake, and may not appreciate the full consequences for a generation. We allowed emotion to obscure logic and belittled anyone who appeared out of step with the current fashion. To marry without good reason is regrettable, to divorce good reasoning from public policy is a disgrace.

In the United States, Same-Sex Couple Households in Massachusetts Are Much Like Heterosexual Families

PR Newswire

PR Newswire delivers news and multimedia content for corporations, public relations firms, and nongovernmental organizations. The Human Rights Campaign is the largest national lesbian and gay political organization in the United States, lobbying Congress, providing campaign support, and educating the public on lesbian, gay, bisexual, and transgender issues. In the following viewpoint, the author reports on U.S. Census Bureau data that reveals similarities between same-sex and heterosexual couple households. The data shows that both types of households raise virtually the same number of children on the same median income. However, the same-sex couple households do not have the same rights for the purposes of taxation and so face higher costs. The author points out that a higher percentage of coupled lesbians serve in the military than their married-women counterparts. While a greater percentage of married men than coupled gay men serve in the military, it is clear that a significant pro-

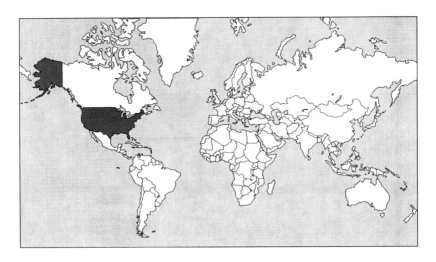

portion of coupled gays and lesbians serve in the military, and yet they do not share the same rights as their married counterparts since they serve under the "Don't ask, don't tell" policy (repealed December 2010).

As you read, consider the following questions:

1. What is the average number of children raised by same-sex couples? By married couples?

2. What is the median personal income in Massachusetts shared by both same-sex and heterosexual couple households?

3. What is the percentage of coupled lesbians versus the percentage of married women serving in the military in Massachusetts? The percentage of coupled gay men versus the percentage of married men serving in the military?

The average Massachusetts family headed by same-sex couples shares many similar characteristics with other families in the state—including number of children being raised and personal income—according to an Urban Institute analysis of newly released Census 2000 data commissioned by the Human Rights Campaign [HRC] Foundation.

"This study should serve as a wake-up call to both state and federal leaders. Families headed by same-sex couples are much more similar to most other families than they are different—and yet too often they don't enjoy the same rights and protections," said HRC Communications Director and Senior Strategist David M. Smith.

"The newly released Census 2000 data provides a detailed portrait of gay and lesbian families that can inform and frame public dialogue about issues that affect all American families," said Gary Gates, Ph.D., of the Urban Institute's population studies center. "It reveals that laws on adoption, marriage, immigration, tax and military service clearly impact all Americans, regardless of sexual orientation."

A 1997 study by the General Accounting Office found that there are more than 1,000 federal rights, responsibilities and obligations associated with marriage that same-sex couples have no access to—many of which are tax related.

The study showed that the average same-sex couple with children in Massachusetts is raising 1.88 children, while the average married couple with children is raising 1.89 children. Yet while the size of families raised by same-sex couples is roughly the same as families headed by heterosexual couples, the number of rights and protections granted to these families is not.

On average, coupled gays and lesbians in Massachusetts have the same median personal income as people who are married—$30,000. However, a 1997 study by the General Accounting Office found that there are more than 1,000 federal rights, responsibilities and obligations associated with marriage that same-sex couples have no access to—many of which are tax related.

The new data supports the arguments contained in a suit brought by the Gay & Lesbian Advocates & Defenders (GLAD) on behalf of seven plaintiff couples in April 2001 seeking the right to civil marriage for same-sex couples in Massachusetts. The case was heard before the state's Supreme Judicial Court in March 2003, and a decision could be released within weeks.

"This case has always been about the state recognizing and treating committed gay and lesbian couples and their children as it does existing married couples and their children," said Mary Bonauto, civil rights director for GLAD and the lead attorney on the case. "Our families have the same concerns every family in Massachusetts shares, and clearly, as this study demonstrates, they operate under the same budget constraints, yet face hundreds of additional costs and taxes simply because they cannot marry. We hope this new data demonstrates that we have much in common with all families in Massachusetts, yet face greater obstacles because we cannot marry."

"Without the legal right to marry, same-sex couples often pay higher taxes for fewer rights than most other Americans. So what looks like equity among partnered gays and lesbians and married couples, may be something else in reality as these couples face disparities in taxation, Social Security benefits, shared property and more," said HRC's Smith.

A dissimilarity the study sheds light on is differences in military service. The study showed that Massachusetts' same-sex coupled women serve their country in the armed forces at significantly higher rates than their married counterparts—6.5 percent of coupled lesbians in Massachusetts have served in the military, compared with only 1.1 percent of married women. The data also shows that 9.3 percent of coupled gay men have served in the military, compared to 29.5 percent of married men.

"Clearly, there are significant numbers of gay men and lesbians serving in the military. It is unconscionable that they should have to serve under a gag order while risking their lives for their country," said Smith. "In fact, these numbers show a substantially higher rate of lesbian women serving in the armed forces than other women—and a significant proportion of gay men—and yet their contribution is marginalized by the deeply insensitive and cruel 'don't ask, don't tell' policy."

"Without the legal right to marry, same-sex couples often pay higher taxes for fewer rights than most other Americans."

The new analyses were drawn from the recently released Census 2000 1% Public Use Microdata Samples (PUMS), a sampling of individual census records from one in 100 U.S. households. The census does not ask questions about sexual orientation. Rather, gay and lesbian families are understood to be households where the respondent identifies another same-sex adult in the house as his or her "husband/wife" or "unmarried partner." Data about the nation's single gay and lesbian population are not available from the census.

Data released on individual states is being released incrementally, and a full report will be completed once data on all states is available.

The Urban Institute is a nonprofit, nonpartisan policy research and educational organization established to examine the social, economic, and governance problems facing the nation. . . .

The Human Rights Campaign is the largest national lesbian and gay political organization with members throughout the country. It effectively lobbies Congress, provides campaign support and educates the public to ensure that lesbian, gay, bisexual and transgender Americans can be open, honest and safe at home, at work and in the community. The Human Rights Campaign Foundation provides public education on issues important to gay, lesbian, bisexual and transgender Americans.

Periodical and Internet Sources Bibliography

The following articles have been selected to supplement the diverse views presented in this chapter.

Annie Guest	"Family Groups to Fight Surrogacy Laws," Australia Broadcasting Corporation, February 12, 2010. www.abc.net.au.
Barry Hatton	"Lesbian Couple Weds in Portugal's First Gay Marriage," PrideSource.com, June 10, 2010. www.pridesource.com.
Jay Makarenko	"Same-Sex Marriage in Canada," Mapleleafweb.com, January 1, 2007. www.mapleleafweb.com.
Andrea Mrozek and Peter Jon Mitchell	"Same-Sex Marriage: Lessons from Canada," Mercatornet.com, September 30, 2008. www.mercatornet.com.
PinkNews	"New South Wales Government Upholds Gay Adoption Ban," January 7, 2010. www.pinknews.co.uk.
Raising Children Network	"Parenting in a Same-Sex Relationship," November 20, 2009. http://raisingchildren.net.au.
B.A. Robinson	"Civil Unions and Same-Sex Marriages in New Zealand," ReligiousTolerance.org, December 10, 2004. www.religioustolerance.org.
Telegraph	"Catholic Adoption Society Seeks Exemption from Gay Rights Legislation," March 3, 2010. www.telegraph.co.uk.
Carin Tiggeloven	"Empty Gesture? Dutch Plans to Expand Same-Sex Adoption Rights," Radio Netherlands Worldwide, March 16, 2005. http://static.rnw.nl.

For Further Discussion

Chapter 1

1. Based on the viewpoints by Hakan Jakob Kosar, Sebastian Moore, and Courage, does Buddhism seem more or less open to homosexuality than Catholicism? Explain your answer.

2. TheReligionofPeace.com argues that the official position of Islam is anti-homosexual but that there is a historical and religious tradition of acceptance of homosexuals. Which of these positions seems to be more important in terms of the treatment of gays in the Islamic nations, according to the viewpoint?

Chapter 2

1. It is sometimes argued that prejudice against homosexuality will lessen over time. Do the viewpoints in this chapter generally support that view, or do they contradict it?

2. Based on the viewpoints by Walter L. Williams, Sudhir Kakar, John Moore, and UNAIDS, is homophobia the result of colonization—that is, did Europeans and Westerners bring it with them to the colonies they conquered? Explain your reasoning.

Chapter 3

1. In his viewpoint, Hossein Derakhshan argues that the makers of a film about transsexuals in Iran mistranslated a key line. Does this mistranslation as he presents it seem like a serious misrepresentation? Of what bias does Derakhshan accuse the filmmakers?

2. Jerry A. Kane writes, "In Canada and European countries, hate crime prosecutions of heterosexuals, non-Muslims, or

non-Socialists exceed those of homosexuals, Muslims, and Socialists." What evidence does he provide for this claim? If the claim is true, does it follow that hate crime laws are unfair? Explain your answer.

Chapter 4

1. Which of Michael Coren's arguments against same-sex marriage does Mercedes Allen specifically address, and are her responses convincing?

2. African Christian Action cites numerous studies that say that gays and/or lesbians are more prone to violence, substance abuse, promiscuity, and other ills. Presuming these studies are true, would they provide a good reason to prevent gay and lesbian couples from adopting? Should other groups that may statistically have higher rates of poverty or criminal incarceration, such as African Americans in the United States, be prevented from adopting as well? Explain your reasoning.

Organizations to Contact

The editors have compiled the following list of organizations concerned with the issues debated in this book. The descriptions are derived from materials provided by the organizations. All have publications or information available for interested readers. The list was compiled on the date of publication of the present volume; the information provided here may change. Be aware that many organizations take several weeks or longer to respond to inquiries, so allow as much time as possible.

American Family Association (AFA)
PO Drawer 2440, Tupelo, MS   38803
(662) 844-5036
website: www.afa.net

A nonprofit organization founded in 1977, the American Family Association (AFA) stands for traditional family values, focusing primarily on the influence of television and other media. Although it works to expose the misrepresentation of radical homosexual rights, AFA also sponsors events reaching out to homosexuals and promoting Christian love and healing. The monthly *AFA Journal* contains news on various moral and family issues. The website offers news, free online newsletters, posters and brochures for downloading, and action alerts.

Africa Christian Action
PO Box 23632, Claremont, Cape Town   7735
   South Africa
(021) 689-4480/1 • fax: (021) 685-5884
e-mail: info@christianaction.org.za
website: www.christianaction.org.za/index.htm

Africa Christian Action mobilizes Christians to make a difference in society and promotes biblical reformation in South Africa. It alerts members to important issues, makes public stands, produces and distributes tracts and newsletters, and engages in education and activism. It opposes homosexual marriage and other gay rights. It publishes the quarterly *Christian Action Magazine*, and its website includes articles such as "Homo-Fascism in South Africa."

Amnesty International USA
5 Penn Plaza, 14th floor, New York, NY   10001
(212) 807-8400 • fax: (212) 627-1451
e-mail: aimember@aiusa.org
website: www.amnestyusa.org

Amnesty International is a worldwide movement of people who campaign for internationally recognized human rights. Its vision is of a world in which every person enjoys all the human rights enshrined in the Universal Declaration of Human Rights and other international human rights standards. The lack of respect, protection, and promotion of the human rights of lesbian, gay, bisexual, and transgender persons is of primary concern to Amnesty International. Each year it publishes a report of its work and its concerns throughout the world. It also publishes numerous individual country reports and briefings, including publications such as "Love, Hate, and the Law: Decriminalizing Homosexuality."

AVERT
4 Brighton Road, Horsham, West Sussex   RF13 5BA
   United Kingdom
+44 (0)1403 210202
e-mail: info@avert.org
website: www.avert.org

The international AIDS charity AVERT works to reduce the number and impact of HIV/AIDS infections globally through education and promotion of positive, proactive treatment of the disease. Many of the organization's projects focus on Africa and India, with an emphasis on prevention as well as aid for those already impacted by AIDS. AVERT's website offers regional summaries of the AIDS epidemic as well as more detailed, specific reports about the prevalence of the disease within particular countries such as South Africa, Malawi, and Uganda. The website also offers resources targeted at gay men and women, such as the booklet *Young Gay Men Talking*.

Dignity USA

PO Box 376, Medford, MA   02155
(800) 877-8797 • fax: (781) 397-0584
e-mail: info@dignityusa.org
website: www.dignityusa.org

Dignity USA is a Catholic organization of gay, lesbian, bisexual, and transgender (GLBT) persons who worship together and advocate for increased GLBT rights within the official church and in American society. Dignity USA publishes a weekly electronic newsletter, *Breath of the Spirit*; a monthly newsletter, *Dateline*; and a membership quarterly, *Quarterly Voice*.

Exodus International

PO Box 540119, Orlando, FL   32854
(888) 264-0877
website: www.exodusinternational.org

Exodus International is a nonprofit, interdenominational Christian organization promoting the message of freedom from homosexuality through the power of Jesus Christ; it is the largest Christian referral and information network dealing with homosexual issues in the world. The group publishes two monthly newsletters, *Exodus Update* and *The Exodus Impact*. Its website offers an online searchable library of articles on aspects of homosexuality from scientific and theological perspectives, first-person accounts from people who have struggled with homosexuality, and downloadable brochures and information.

Gay and Lesbian Rights Lobby

PO Box 304, Glebe NSW   2037
   Australia

(02) 9571-5501 • fax: (02) 9571-5509
website: http://glrl.org.au

The Gay & Lesbian Rights Lobby (GLRL) is an Australian organization that advocates on behalf of lesbians and gay men. It provides referral and educative resources on gay and lesbian rights to the media, policy makers, and the community. Its website includes press releases and numerous publications, including "Submission to the Inquiry into Adoption by Same-Sex Couples" and "From Lives of Fear to Lives of Freedom: A Review of Australian Refugee Decisions on the Basis of Sexual Orientation."

Human Rights Watch
350 Fifth Avenue, 34th Floor, New York, NY   10118-3299
(212) 290-4700
website: www.hrw.org

Founded in 1978, Human Rights Watch is a nongovernmental organization that conducts systematic investigations of human rights abuses in countries around the world. It opposes discrimination against homosexuals. It publishes many books and reports on specific countries and issues as well as annual reports and other articles, such as "Burundi: Repeal Law Criminalizing Homosexual Conduct" and "Uganda: 'Anti-Homosexuality' Bill Threatens Liberties and Human Rights Defenders."

ReligiousTolerance.org
OCRT, Box 27026, Kingston, ON
  K7M 8W5
  Canada
fax: (888) 806-6115
e-mail: ocrtfeedback@gmail.com
website: www.religioustolerance.org

ReligiousTolerance.org is an online multi-faith group whose mission is to explain the full diversity of religious beliefs in North America. The website, maintained by the Ontario Consultants on Religious Tolerance, attempts to describe all viewpoints on controversial religious topics objectively and fairly; issues include whether homosexuals and bisexuals should be given equal rights, including same-sex marriage. The site also offers an online forum, lists of recommended books, and links to other religious sites.

UNAIDS

Analysis and Programme Development, 20 Avenue Appia
Geneva 27   CH-1211
  Switzerland
+41.22.791.3666 • fax: +41.22.791.4187
website: www.unaids.org

UNAIDS, or the Joint United Nations Programme on HIV/ Aids, is an agency of the United Nations that promotes efforts to internationally combat the AIDS epidemic. The organization focuses its efforts into areas such as prevention, treatment, and care; populations most affected by the disease; the broader effects of the disease on communities; and general research into vaccines and preventive measures. UNAIDS has published numerous documents detailing all aspects of this global disease, with most reports in its extensive catalog available on its website in portable document format.

Bibliography of Books

M.V. Lee Badgett — *When Gay People Get Married: What Happens When Societies Legalize Same-Sex Marriage.* New York: New York University Press, 2009.

Javier Corrales and Mario Pecheny, eds. — *The Politics of Sexuality in Latin America: A Reader on Lesbian, Gay, Bisexual, and Transgender Rights.* Pittsburgh, PA: University of Pittsburgh Press, 2010.

Louis Crompton — *Homosexuality & Civilization.* Cambridge, MA: Harvard University Press, 2003.

Marc Epprecht — *Heterosexual Africa? The History of an Idea from the Age of Exploration to the Age of AIDS.* Athens: Ohio University Press, 2008.

Rudolf Pell Gaudio — *Allah Made Us: Sexual Outlaws in an Islamic African City.* Malden, MA: Wiley-Blackwell, 2009.

Samar Habib, ed. — *Islam and Homosexuality.* Santa Barbara, CA: Praeger, 2010.

Stephen Hicks and Jane McDermott, eds. — *Lesbian and Gay Fostering and Adoption: Extraordinary Yet Ordinary.* Philadelphia, PA: Jessica Kingsley Publishers, 1999.

Neville Hoad — *African Intimacies: Race, Homosexuality and Globalization.* Minneapolis: University of Minnesota Press, 2007.

Thomas Hopko — *Christian Faith and Same-Sex Attraction: Eastern Orthodox Reflections.* Ben Lomond, CA: Conciliar Press, 2006.

Peter A. Jackson and Gerard Sullivan, eds. — *Lady Boys, Tom Boys, Rent Boys: Male and Female Homosexualities in Contemporary Thailand.* New York: Harrington Park Press, 1999.

James B. Jacobs and Kimberly Potter — *Hate Crimes: Criminal Law & Identity Politics.* New York: Oxford University Press, 1998.

Mark D. Jordan — *The Silence of Sodom: Homosexuality in Modern Catholicism.* Chicago, IL: University of Chicago Press, 2000.

Scott Siraj al-Haqq Kugle — *Homosexuality in Islam: Islamic Reflection on Gay, Lesbian, and Transgender Muslims.* Oxford, UK: Oneworld Publications, 2010.

Winston Leyland, ed. — *Queer Dharma: Voices of Gay Buddhists, Volume 2.* San Francisco, CA: Gay Sunshine Press, 2000.

Jonathan D. Mackintosh — *Homosexuality and Manliness in Postwar Japan.* New York: Routledge, 2010.

Mark J. McLelland — *Male Homosexuality in Modern Japan: Cultural Myths and Social Realities.* Richmond, UK: Curzon Press, 2000.

Yuval Merin

Equality for Same-Sex Couples: The Legal Recognition of Gay Partnerships in Europe and the United States. Chicago, IL: University of Chicago Press, 2002.

Gary Mucciaroni

Same Sex, Different Politics: Success and Failure in the Struggles over Gay Rights. Chicago, IL: University of Chicago Press, 2008.

Kerry H. Robinson, Jude Irwin, Tania Ferfolia, eds.

From Here to Diversity: The Social Impact of Lesbian and Gay Issues in Education in Australia and New Zealand. New York: Harrington Park Press, 2002.

Jeremy Seabrook

Love in a Different Climate: Men Who Have Sex with Men in India. New York: Verso, 1999.

Melinda Selmys

Sexual Authenticity: An Intimate Reflection on Homosexuality and Catholicism. Huntington, IN: Our Sunday Visitor, 2009.

Parmesh Shahani

Gay Bombay: Globalization, Love and (Be)longing in Contemporary India. Thousand Oaks, CA: SAGE Publications, 2008.

Miriam Catherine Smith

Political Institutions and Lesbian and Gay Rights in the United States and Canada. New York: Routledge, 2008.

Andrew Sullivan, ed.

Same-Sex Marriage, Pro and Con: A Reader. New York: Vintage Books, 2004.

Phillip Tahmindjis and Helmut Graupner, eds.

Sexuality and Human Rights: A Global Overview. New York: Harrington Park Press, 2005.

Index

Geographic headings and page numbers in **boldface** refer to viewpoints about that country or region.